Daylight

THE MANY PLEASURES

Found Art in New York City

BARTON LEWIS

Cofounders: Taj Forer and Michael Itkoff
Creative Director: Ursula Damm
Copy Editor: Gabrielle Fastman

ISBN: 978-1-954119-40-6

Printed by Ofset Yapimevi, Turkey

Daylight Books
E-mail: info@daylightbooks.org
Web: www.daylightbooks.org

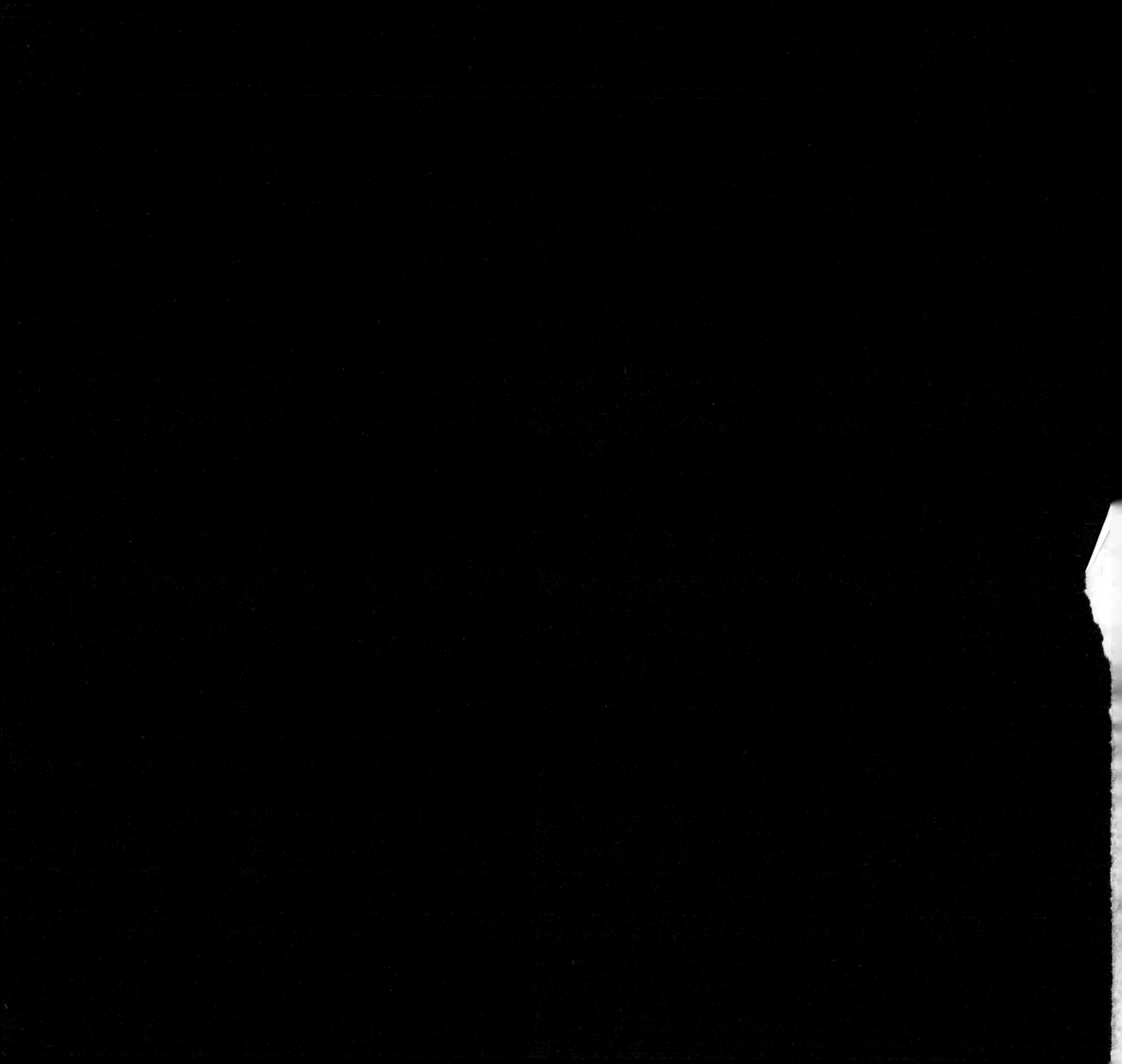

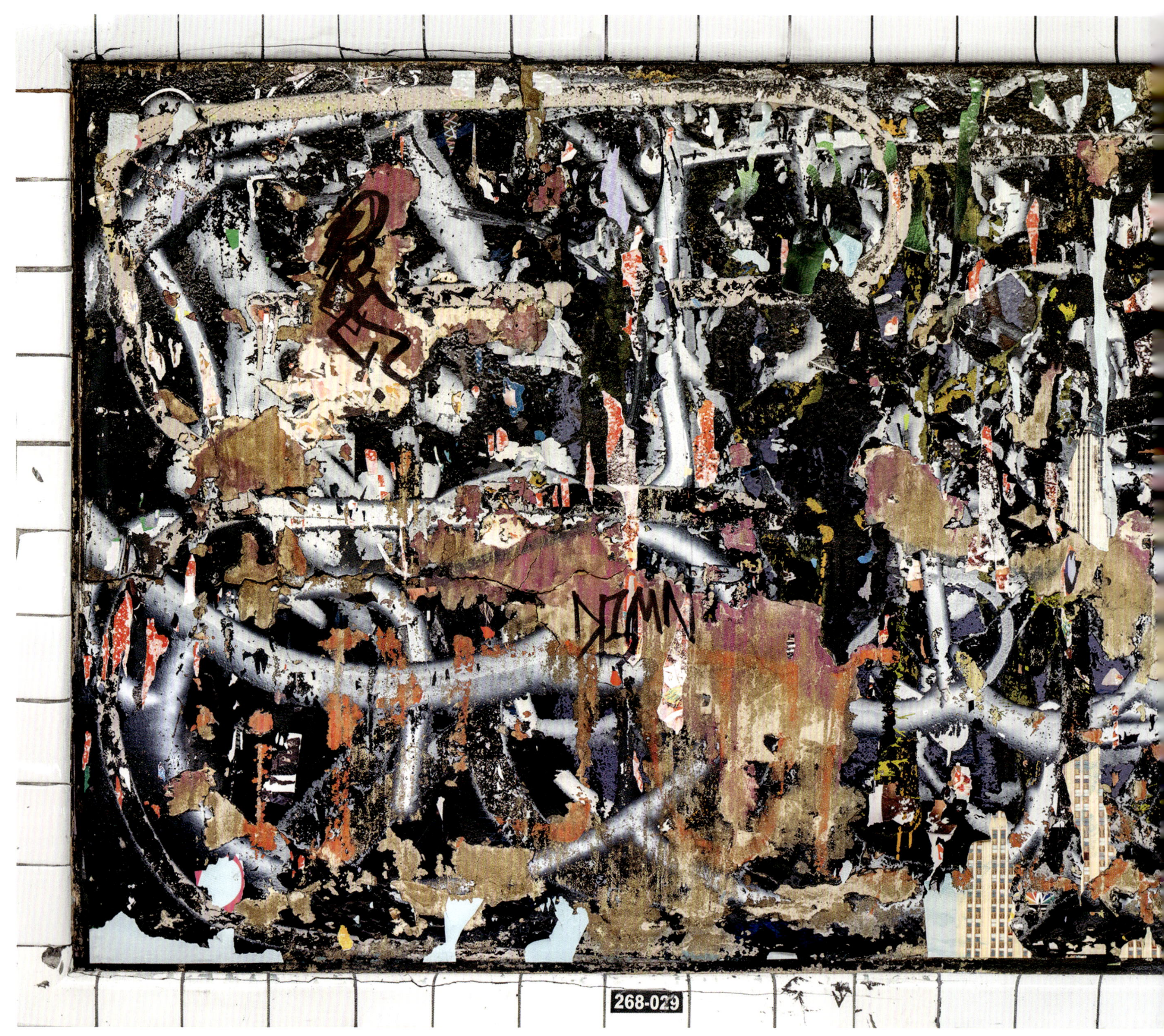
268-029

Schneeman screened and/or edited their independent films there. The film begins with highly abstract posters, leavings speckled in the expressive old glue palette of yellow, gray, and muddy black. Occasional gobs of poster paper resolutely hang on. In other shots, we witness more deliberate slashing. A basketball hero's head looms large over dramatic tears in a poster that includes a sticker reading "Broken Guru." Meanwhile, the live soundtrack features wheezing brakes, clacking train arrivals, incoherent conductor announcements, and shards of conversation like "I love you," echoing as the subway train leaves the station. The film presages key themes of the photographs in *The Many Pleasures*, which Lewis has been capturing since 2018.

Lewis explains, "A collector suggested doing still photography as a large-scale subgenre of the moving image." And indeed, we do the moving on the street and the imagery is still. The artist has curated the still images in *The Many Pleasures* "intuitively, based on what looks best." On his scouting expeditions, people often ask what he's doing, including the police. One time he was crouched behind his camera as light hit a Bushwick building just right. A patrol-car window rolled down and a policeman asked what he was doing. "Oh, you're an artist," he responded, after Lewis briefly explained, and drove off.

This marvelous eavesdropping on the visual unfolds in sumptuous images, often sewn together digitally from multiple shots. "I composite each wall cut from approximately twelve to eighteen shots," he says. "Larger images can involve considerably more." Some of the subway wall cuts stretch fourteen feet or more. At times Lewis stitches ad-covered columns into a forest of pillars. On occasion he has peeled some paper himself, but mostly his images document the alternation between random weathering and deliberate interventions by anonymous urban artists.

ADVERTISING

The project reminds us how New Yorkers gleefully seize opportunities to remake their surroundings, and how these intentionally shredded posters may function as a rejoinder to commercial messaging in public space. The interventions claim public space as a public good. Madison Avenue may rent the space, but regular citizens can elect to work their aesthetic urges on this public canvas too.

Lewis makes us aware of the layered rhetoric of advertising, how weaponized language and icons are deployed to persuade and open wallets. Advertising originated as a layered language of culture symbols. But the symbolic language of ads operates in public space, where commercial aims may be bent to other, more free-spirited expressions. Both natural deterioration and the deliberate slicing of ads underline the metaphoric energy of these palimpsests. Take for example his image of a

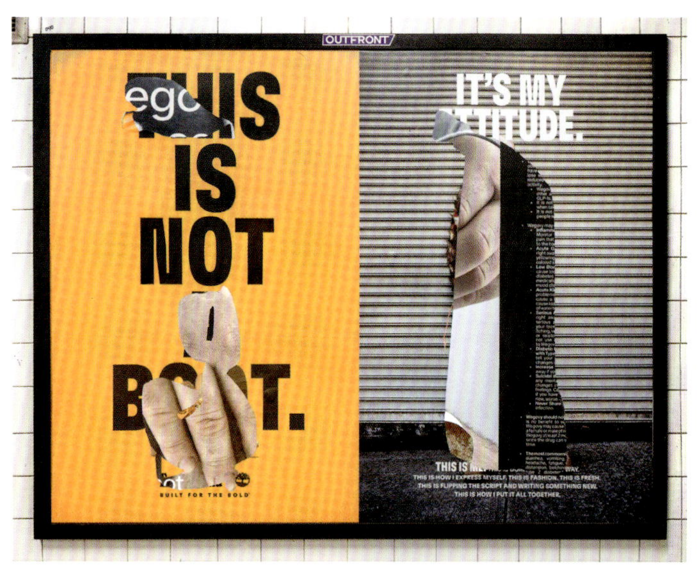

OUTFRONT
THIS IS NOT A BOOT.
IS NOT BOOT.
BUILT FOR THE BOLD
IT'S MY ATTITUDE.
THIS IS ME. THIS IS DONE MY WAY.
THIS IS HOW I EXPRESS MYSELF. THIS IS FASHION. THIS IS FRESH.
THIS IS FLIPPING THE SCRIPT AND WRITING SOMETHING NEW.
THIS IS HOW I PUT IT ALL TOGETHER.

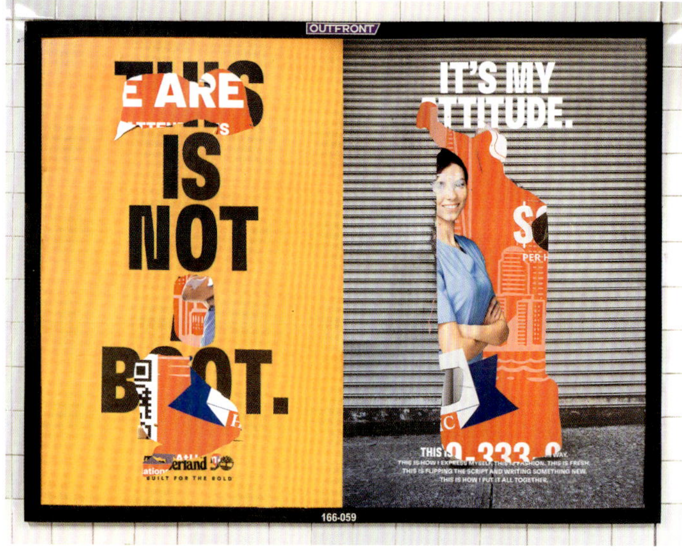

OUTFRONT
THIS IS NOT A BOOT.
E ARE
IS NOT BOOT.
BUILT FOR THE BOLD
IT'S MY ATTITUDE.
$0 PER H
THIS IS HOW I EXPRESS MYSELF. THIS IS FASHION. THIS IS FRESH.
THIS IS FLIPPING THE SCRIPT AND WRITING SOMETHING NEW.
THIS IS HOW I PUT IT ALL TOGETHER.
166-059

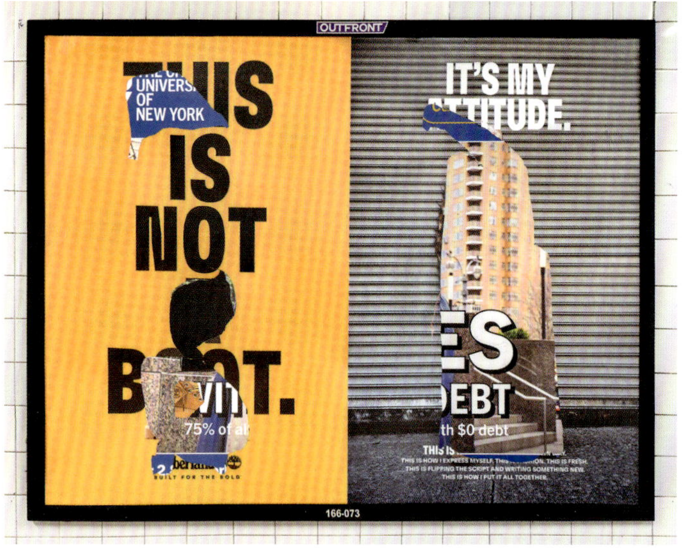

OUTFRONT
THIS IS NOT A BOOT.
THE CI
UNIVERSITY OF
NEW YORK
IS NOT BOOT.
75% of al
BUILT FOR THE BOLD
IT'S MY ATTITUDE.
ES
DEBT
th $0 debt
THIS IS
THIS IS HOW I EXPRESS MYSELF. THIS IS FASHION. THIS IS FRESH.
THIS IS FLIPPING THE SCRIPT AND WRITING SOMETHING NEW.
THIS IS HOW I PUT IT ALL TOGETHER.
166-073

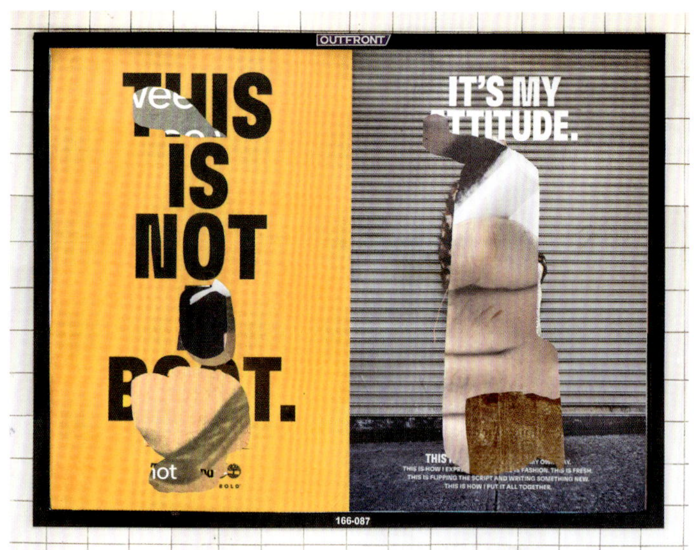

OUTFRONT
THIS IS NOT A BOOT.
IS NOT BOOT.
BUILT FOR THE BOLD
IT'S MY ATTITUDE.
THIS
THIS IS HOW I EXP
THIS IS FLIPPING THE SCRIPT AND WRITING SOMETHING NEW.
THIS IS HOW I PUT IT ALL TOGETHER.
166-087

building facade entitled *10th St. between 3rd & 4th Aves. no. 1, New York, NY* (p. 33). In the nine-by-nine set of images, a street artist has artfully reclothed and re-posed models as oblong abstractions, the images sequential but completely unrecognizable as the work of a named fashion designer. It has now truly become an "exclusive Collection." The artist seems to be cutting paper dolls onto the sleek surface of the ad, acts that proclaim no one owns fashion.

New Yorkers' visual gifts and propensity to acts of public unruliness feed on the creative output of the advertising industry. Public space has its own codes of visual language. The refined iconic elements of outdoor advertising—meant for ingesting in gulps—must be very bold, simple, direct, much less language based than print ads. This distilled iconic language becomes something wild and free in the hands of poster slashers who create daggers of color and wacky juxtapositions of figures, sometimes leaving clues to the original in tiny bites of text. These interventions uncover advertising genealogies, a whiff of history embedded in the ephemeral. The ads seduce us with visual treats to buy stuff that ends up on the junk heaps of consumer culture, nearly as fast as the outdoor advertising itself shreds. If outdoor advertising speaks a language of exuberant commercialism, it also reminds us of the decline and fall of cultural moments. These eloquent remnants, like *wall cut, 268-025 – 268-029, 65th St., IND Queens Blvd. Line, Queens, NY* (p. 4) may be memento mori, testifying to the flaky obsolescence of the outpourings of Madison Avenue.

GRAFFITI AND APPROPRIATION ART

Lewis invites us to consider these displays as a genre of appropriation art. If art is often the act of perception, then New Yorkers seem determined to make us see our surroundings in new ways. At a deep level, these interventions assert the priority of people in public space. They draw nourishment from an implicit notion that the community owns the collective look of a space. While not the actual property holders, as residents we have rights to the ensemble of how architecture, landscaping, business activity, and even dilapidation come together as the urban look. This visual sense of place results from massive human inputs, adding up to more than just design—it's the face of our urban fabric. These notions of collective visual rights trace their ancestry to the City Beautiful movement, which supported the idea that we all have a stake in how the city looks. Furthermore, these concepts about visuality formed the basis for laws regulating billboards back in the early twentieth century and underpin the reasoning behind the public interest in limiting shadows, planning tall buildings, and protecting historic neighborhoods.

The widespread guerrilla actions that form the core of Lewis's series deploy walls, fences, and mailboxes as urban sketchbooks. The nocturnal expeditions of rip-and-tear artists see advertisements as provocations temporarily glued to the world: like their interventions, neither original nor altered ad will stick around long. Performed as stealth aesthetics, this so-called "vandalism" slices through a jungle of prohibitions and unfolds as sequential unknown collaborations between individuals who agree that they, too, have a right to cumulative creation and public presence. Urban guerilla art stirs the pot with a belief that the destruction of the original may be a boldly modernist act of creation.

PROCESS

"I love the flavor of impermanence and transition that I find in these objects," says Lewis. His photographic project shows how the phenomena of outdoor ads, with their combinations of accidental and intended, are a kind of process art. Imagery mutates: new ads and graffiti stickers are added and layers, color saturation, imagery, fading texts are subtracted. During these transformations, ownership and authorship are destabilized. Shredding represents the decline and fall of miniature episodes of civilization, slowly cascading into oblivion.

Sometimes decay itself arrests our attention. For example, *wall cut, Casino, 103rd St., IND Eighth Ave. Line, New York, NY* (p. 108), advertising Martin Scorsese's 1995 film, has lingered for over twenty-three years. Cold, damp, wind, and time have scrubbed off most of the imagery, leaving traces of an old transit map, still legible when Lewis documented the hearty survivor in 2018.

Mother Nature has more thoroughly scoured *wall cut, 162-143 – 162-147, 50th St., IND Eighth Ave. Line, New York, NY* (p. 103), leaving behind something like yellowed reptile skin, the pleasures of craquelure patterns extending three panels wide. This mural functions like a reverie of passing, the skin of our visual language being shed. This weathered set of ads reminds us that much urban experience draws on corner-of-the-eye perception, subtle effects that we imbibe unconsciously as we pass through various spaces. Sometimes the experience engages the foreground and background of perception, as if we imaginatively pass right through a two-dimensional thing. In that manner these works resonate with Sam Gilliam's hangings, which dissolve the foreground and background categories of seeing.

Sometimes the gabby walls seem to buttonhole us in a conversation. The images pinpoint the way art is a conversation, an exchange between what's visible and how we perceive things. Truncated ad slogans change significance as judicious slicing maroons them in new contexts. These textual bits have the allure of encounters with random strangers. Look, for instance, at *wall cut, 029-069, 4th Ave. & 9th St., BMT Fourth Ave. Line, Brooklyn, NY* (p. 117). Near elegant vertical layers arranged by a box-cutter artist, another passerby has wryly scribbled, "She's texting someone else, bro, move on." Or consider how the words "hangover delivered," visible on bright blue, anchor a stomach-churning expanse of mottled gray and brown in *wall cut, 322-069 14th St.-6th Ave., New York, NY* (p. 112) at Union Square—a location where many a drifter swigs liquor in the park overhead. We feel reality leaking all over the place.

The streetscape is intriguing, full of mystery where processions of torn imagery trigger associations and reveries. *The Many Pleasures* invites the viewer to surrender to narrative fantasy. So, for example, we might detect a mighty ocean battle in *wall cut, 260-361, 75th Ave., IND Queens Blvd. Line, Queens, NY* (p. 116). A maelstrom of swirling blueish confetti suggests a watery monster thrashing; could it be the whale gobbling Jonah? Sometimes the ads are so weathered that we sense something trying to crawl out from the tattered surface: a face, a glance, a word? Indeed, in the fretful shards of the grand abstraction *wall cut, 237-207 – 237-211, Carroll St., IND Culver Line, Brooklyn, NY* (p. 89) we can discover in tiny letters "Bill de [Blasio]." In *wall cut, 229-283, 14th St.-6th Ave., New York, NY* (p. 79) ominous text snippets—"chat blood misuse bank"—polka dot a vertically slashed array of punchy red, lavender, and hot pink.

In some cases, the weathering produces compositions that seem to echo art traditions. In *wall cut, 243-205, Church Ave., IND Culver Line, Brooklyn,* *NY* (p. 72) the eye follows an ascending zig-zag path up a mountain. These spectral remains hint at a spiritual journey on water or through mountains, as in the Chinese tradition of shan shui brush-and-ink paintings, whose elusive contours and wobbly perspective reflect thoughts about nature, not nature itself.

Lewis's project constitutes a chapter in a longer international art history. Some French artists in the 1950s responded to Paris's poster-rich streets with acts of creative vandalism, scraping giant billboards off walls and then excavating layers, often from the back. Jacques Villeglé and Raymond Hains toyed with the onomatopoeic potential of fragments and syllables, which appeared even more mysterious when seen in reverse and upside down on their purloined fragments. Mimmo Rotella in Italy particularly relished the effects of deterioration and used torn posters to create new works of "décollage." His fragmented interpretations of flayed movie posters commented on the machinery of celebrity, as well as the pop qualities of giant scale. Like Rotella, the French *afŞchiste* François Dufrêne was a poet interested in typographic deformations, a movement called Lettrism. These themes are an undercurrent in the history of street art that connect artists with such social critics as Guy Debord, author of *The Society of Spectacle* and inventor of situationism, a dissident response to advertising's attempted colonization of our brains. Likewise, the slashers of New York outdoor advertising proudly treat the walls as an invitation to aesthetic mischief that disrupts advertising messages. As Walter Benjamin would see it, the commodity brims with poetic content, despite its crass purposes.

SPACES

Benjamin, that superb interpreter of city life, wrote that "art teaches us to see into things." Lewis, too, understands the poetic potential of beleaguered urban spaces. Saturated with commodity culture, they nevertheless yield up aesthetic riches to the sensitive observer. Building-site fences, customarily painted a bucolic green, bring a tropical luxuriance to spaces often bereft of flora. Even in decay these saturated greens can suggest the persistence of nature, under the commercial messaging. In *construction fence, 44th St. & Madison Ave., New York, NY* (p. 22), scraping has left fronds dangling over what looks like a garden party of ladies in kimonos.

In *construction fence, Berry St. between S. 2nd & S. 3rd Sts., Brooklyn, NY* (p. 29), advertising for a facial mask produced by Youth to the People offers uplifting slogans like "No Walls, Just Dreams," and "Less Hate, Just Hydrate." These nostrums grab the attention but cannot adhere to the product, Superberry Hydrate and Glow Dream Mask. Urban strollers may be skeptical about the promised radiance and plumping but happy with the ample blank spaces that invite artful tearing.

Lewis also pauses in his city ramblings to honor stoic US postal relay boxes, often sporting dense layers of stickers and graffiti. The squat structures calmly endure repeated assaults with Sharpie, X-acto knife, and brush. In one, a mailbox repainted pink bears the moniker "Traitor" crying out amidst abstract strokes of color under the evil glare of a blue-faced demon. On another a glamor gal's outlined chest consists of the clawed remnants of an earlier layer of red-and-pink posting. An impudent remake of the Quaker Oats man gives him hipster sunglasses. The redecoration of these relentless utilitarian structures gives voice to city style.

Many neglected or abandoned buildings have been reduced to giant poster stands, and these Warhol-esque multiples can be seen as critiques of brainwashing and the flood tide of advertising. Lewis created a monumental tribute to this genre with his *156 Levi's ads, Banker & N. 15th Sts., Brooklyn, NY* (p. 41). He painstakingly stitched together 152 photographs to capture the relentless repetitions. We don't need to see any jeans; "501" suffices to trigger user memories of the classic five-pocket button-fly originals. Weathering has lacerated the posters into individual ghosts of their former selves, a procession that extends sixty-five feet. The phenomenon of large unoccupied industrial buildings reduced to marketing space speaks to how cycles of decay can make the once solid city seem like a movie set of forlorn facades.

Two studies of I-beams holding up subway stations also suggest how infrastructure dresses up as something else. The series photographed at Union Square station (p. 17) seem to comb the waves of commuters diverging on either side of the posts. Calling for help on the Galaxy S8 phone advertised on the column may not help as viral orange-red rust climbs like vines determined to take down the entire built environment. Similarly, the I-beams photographed at the Bedford Ave. station in Brooklyn (p. 65), set in a gleaming modernist environment of chrome steps and steel pipes, appear as ornate as pillars in a Roman temple but ready to crumble soon, along with the empire, as paint chips, paper shreds, and metal rusts.

UNKNOWN AUTHORSHIP

These anonymous artists, night walkers with paint scrapers and flashlights, hide from us. And yet some examples offer clear proof of individual artistic production. Like the Paleolithic cave paintings of Lascaux, we don't know the author, but we can read their skilled intentions in the artwork. In the four wall cuts photographed at the 14th St.-8th Ave. subway station (p. 9), someone scratched a mysterious set of figures, obliterating the Timberland boots models to take us to a much more enigmatic zone. Shot against a corrugated gate used to protect stores from riots and looting, a textured backdrop connoting urbanity, the steel in this ad series turns into a palette of fashion. The variations all peel back a distinct portion, conforming to an overall shape. And the slogans left readable fit the alterations: "This is not a boot, it's my attitude." Elsewhere the ad copy reads "this is how I express myself." Much of the audience will recognize famous figures posing in Timberlands—boots popular with rappers and celebrities, which have inspired open-toed platform-soled iterations and Manolo Blahnik variations in stiletto worn by Jennifer Lopez and Rihanna, among others. So the canny artist in this case runs with the mandate for self-expression to scrape off celebrity and substitute figures and abstractions uncovered in earlier layers of ads.

CONCLUSION

Lewis's photographic journey through New Yorkers' rip, tear, and mark rebellion affirms the anarchic energy of urban street art. From witty excavation to gob-smacking overwriting, *The Many Pleasures* invites us to engage with urban poetics and decode the city's soul. Playing peekaboo with the everyday, these tattered remnants scratch through to the other side of reality where the unseen and the imagined are more desirable than the legible.

on the street

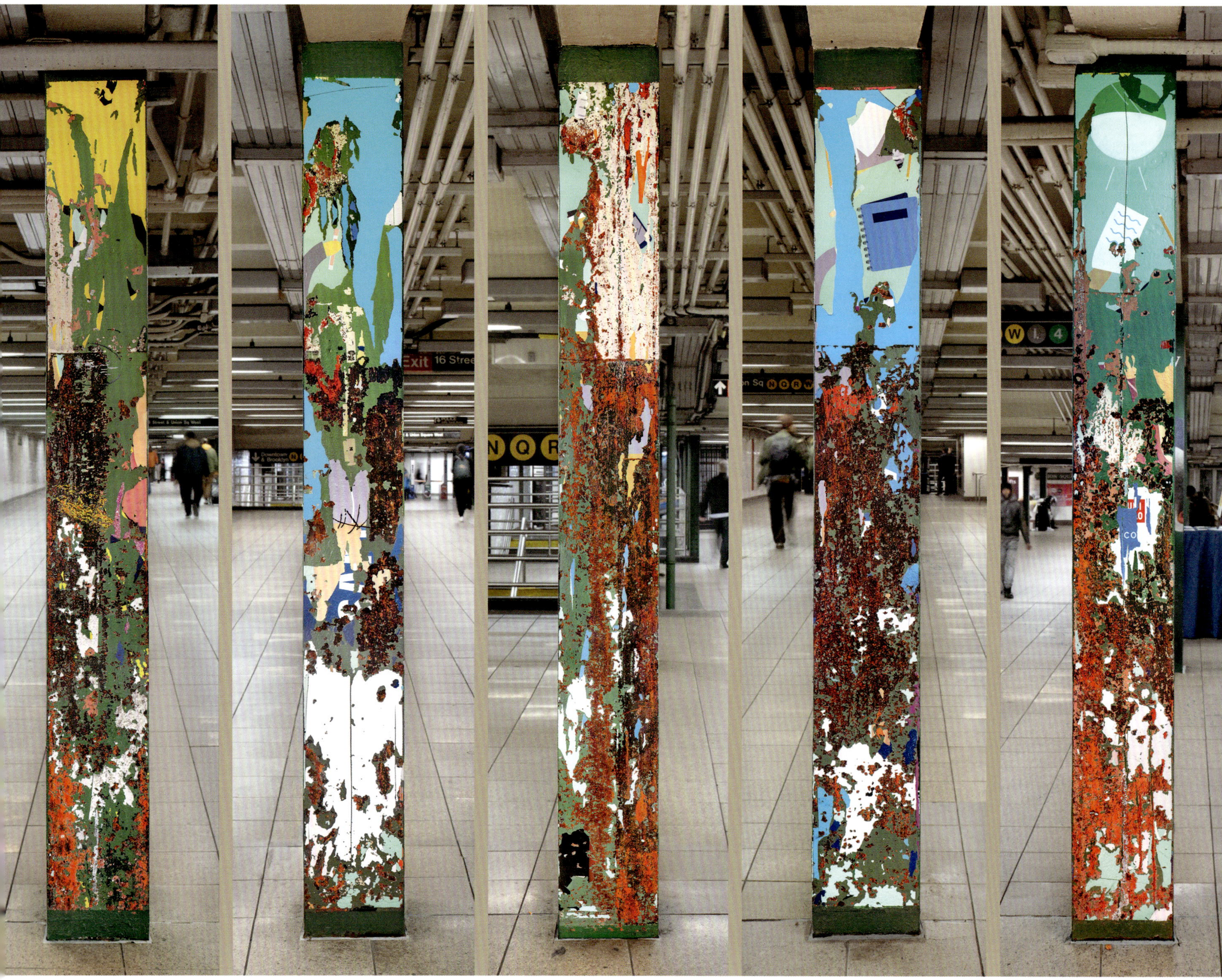

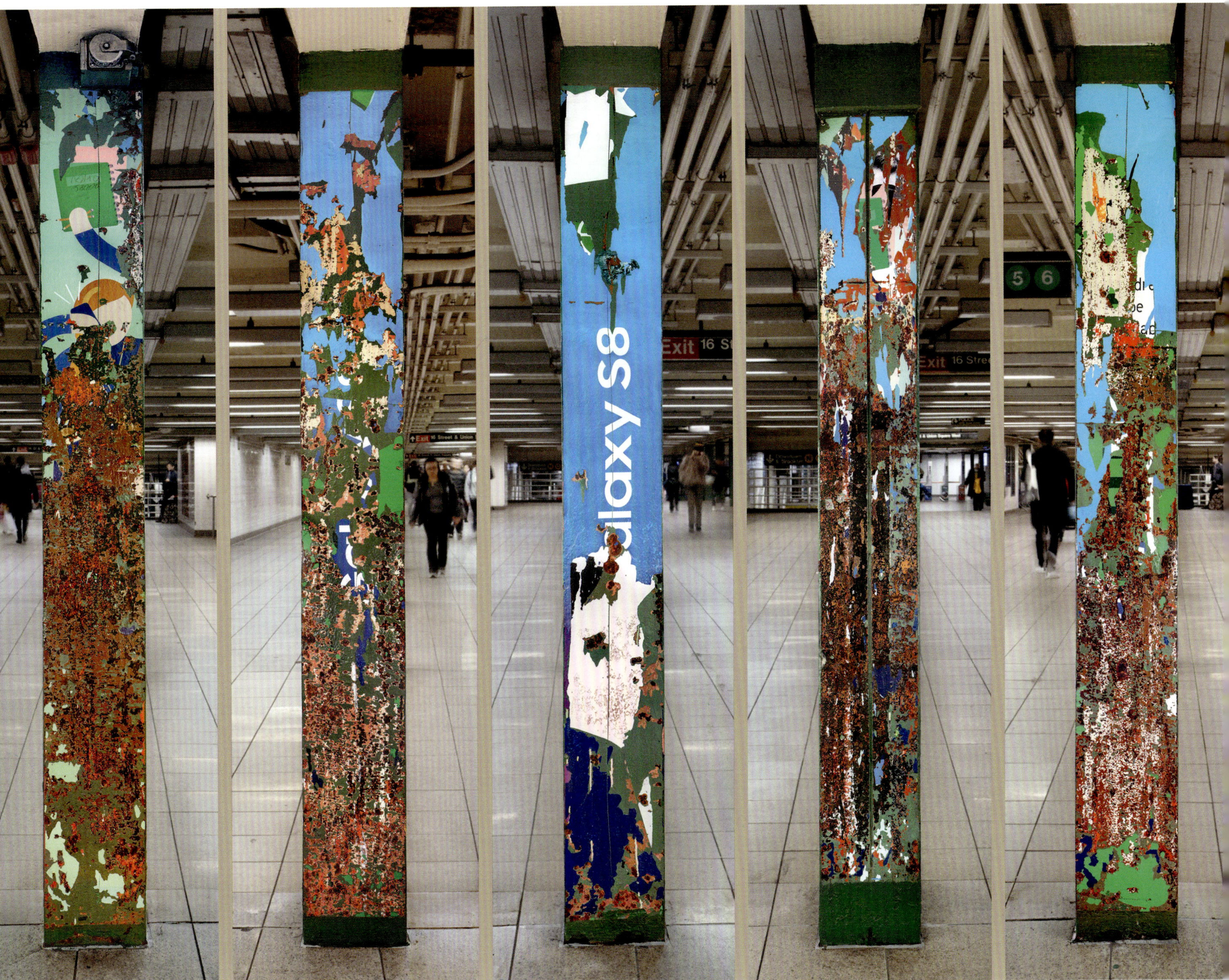

alaxy S8
Exit 16 St
Exit 16 Street
5 6

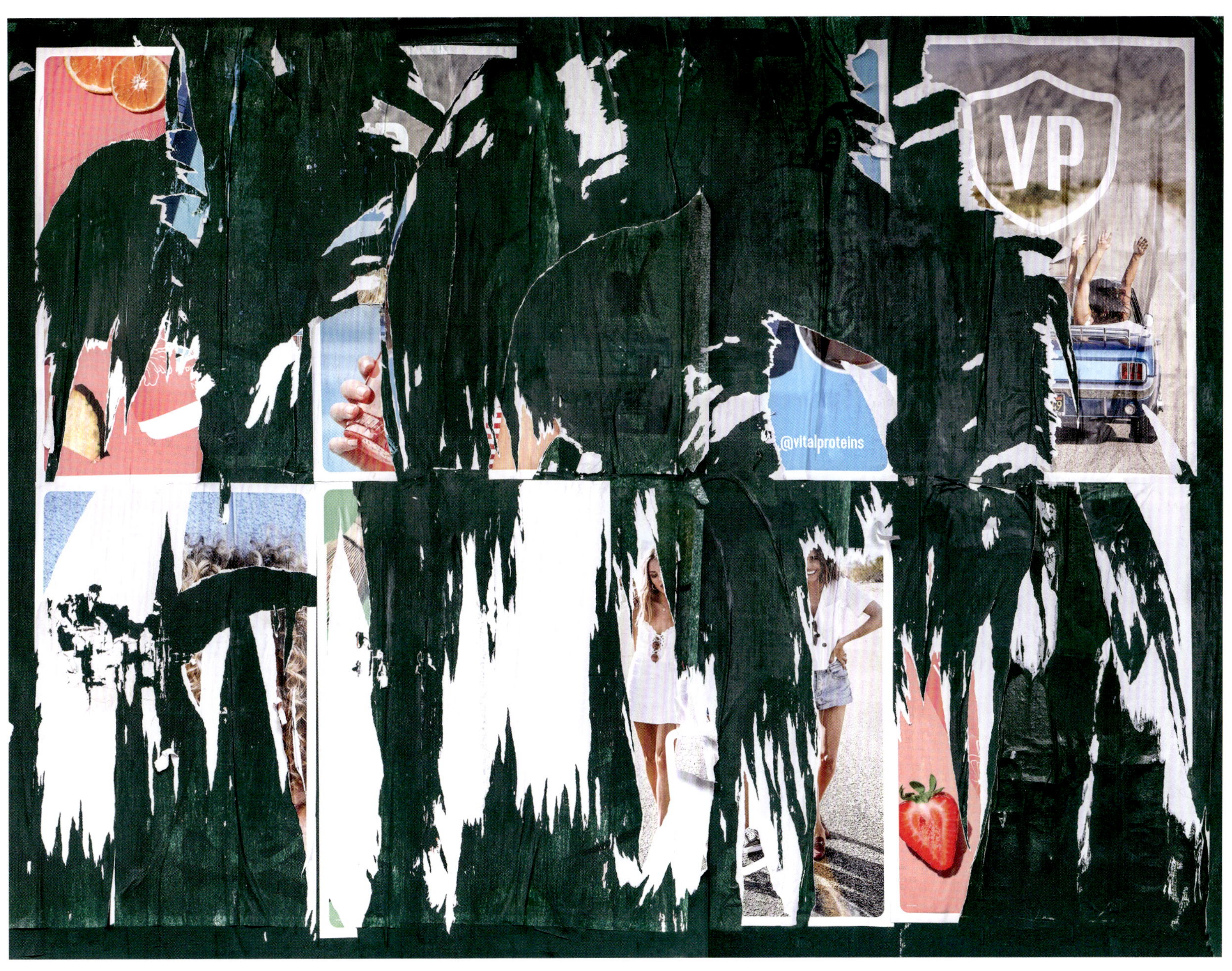

VP
@vitalproteins

HUDSON YA
HUDSON YARDS SPRING 2019

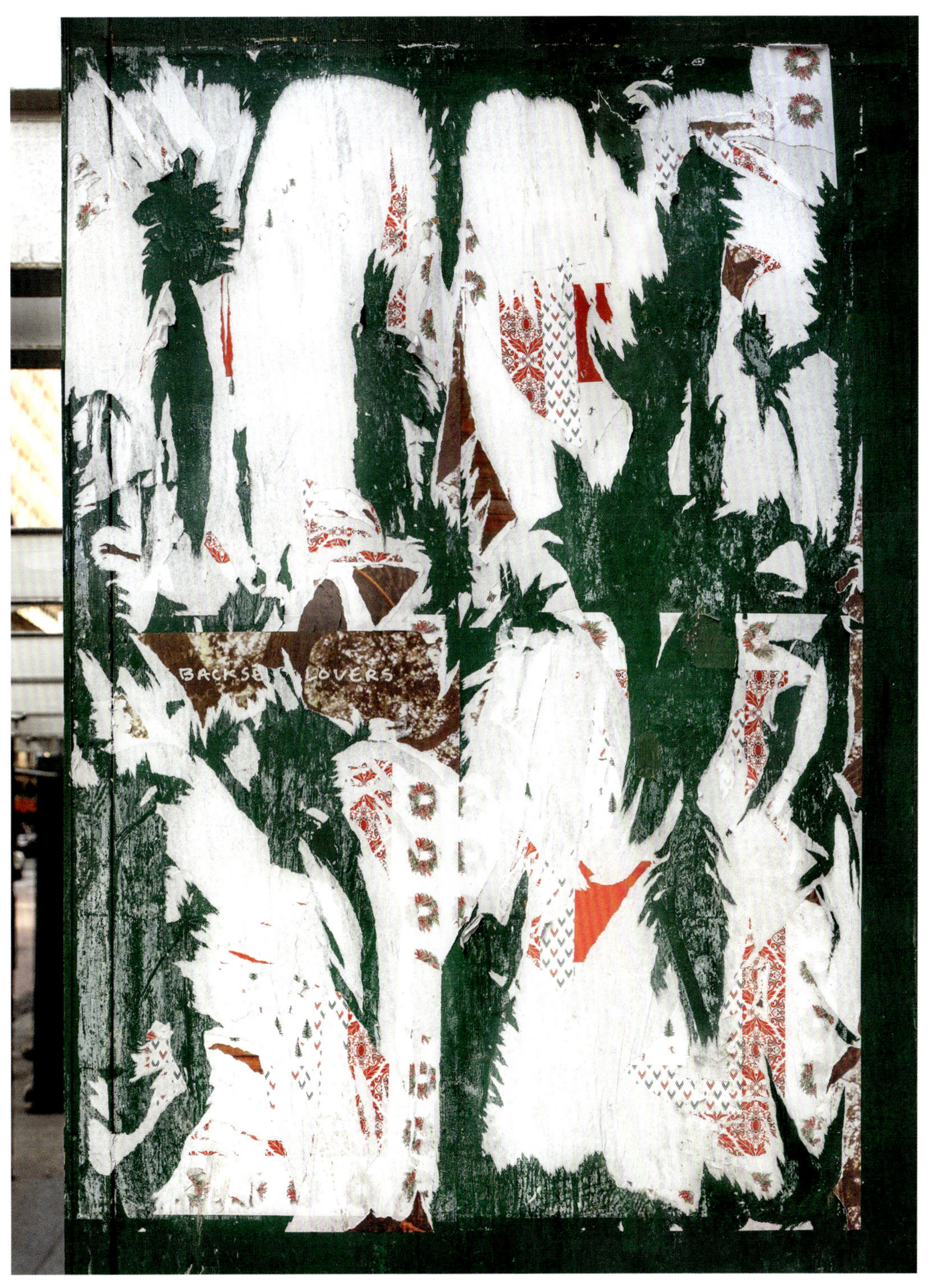

BACKSEAT LOVERS

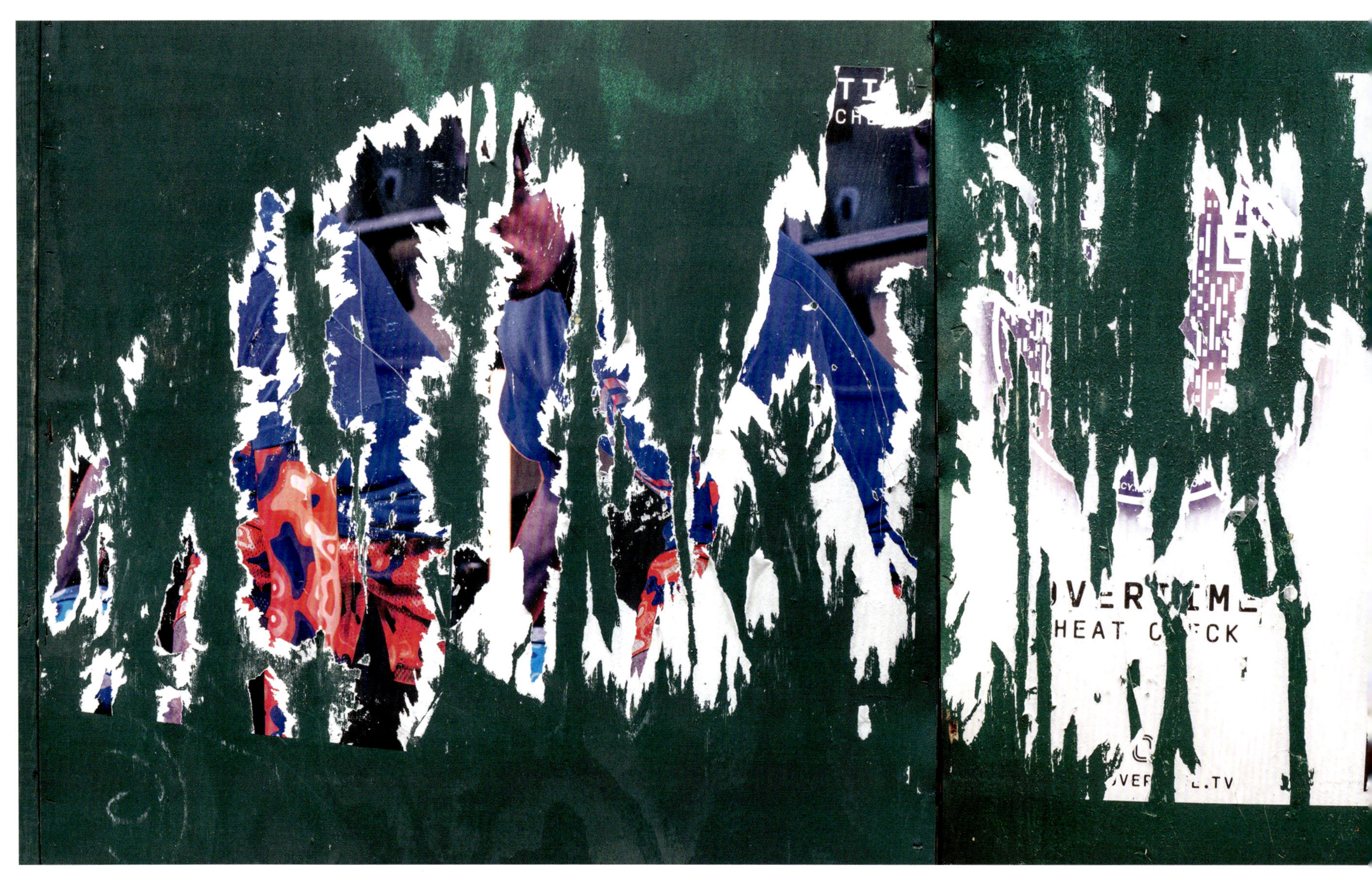
OVERTIME
HEAT CHECK
OVERTIME.TV

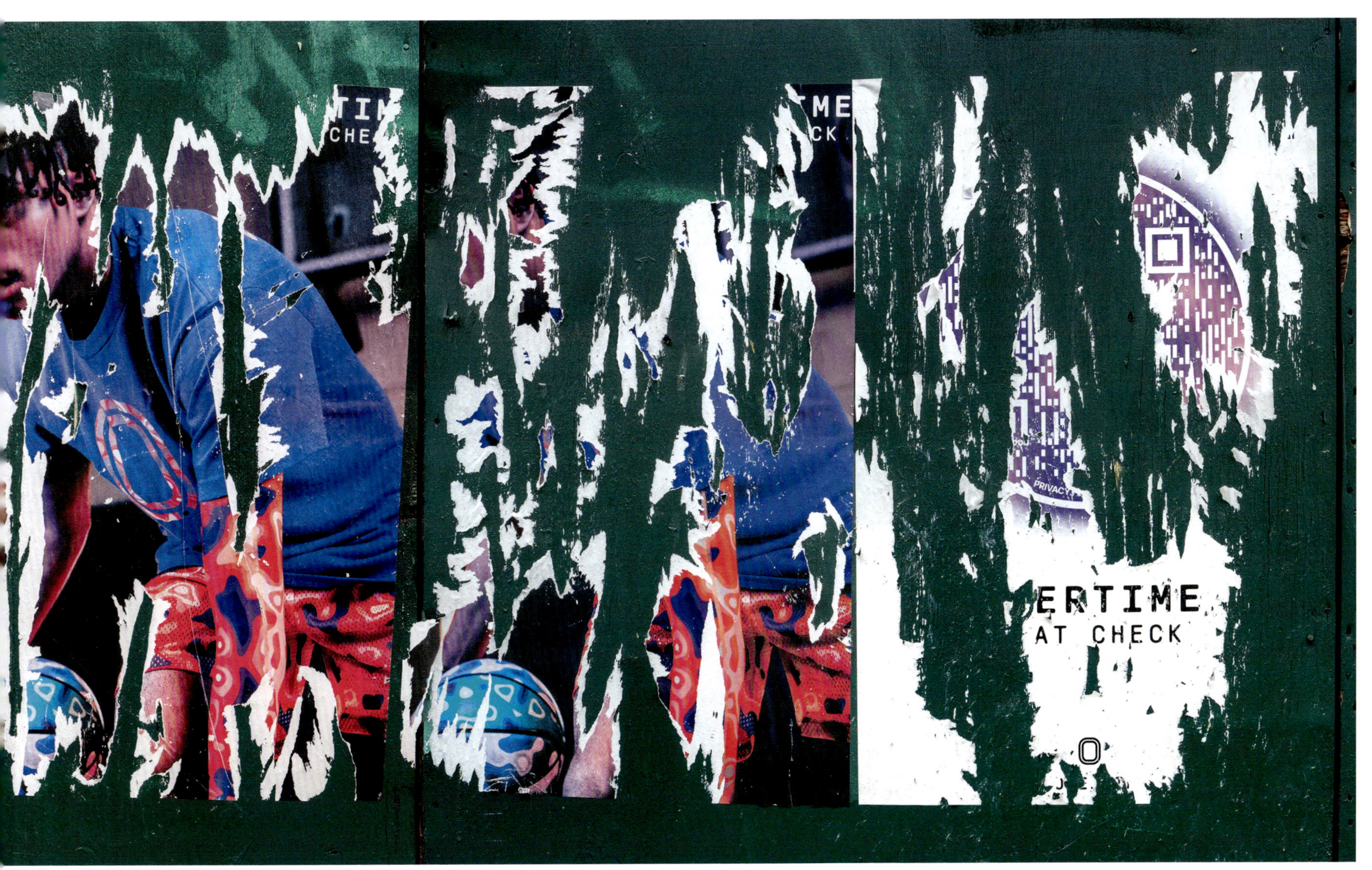
TIM
CHE
ME
CK
PRIVACY
ERTIME
AT CHECK

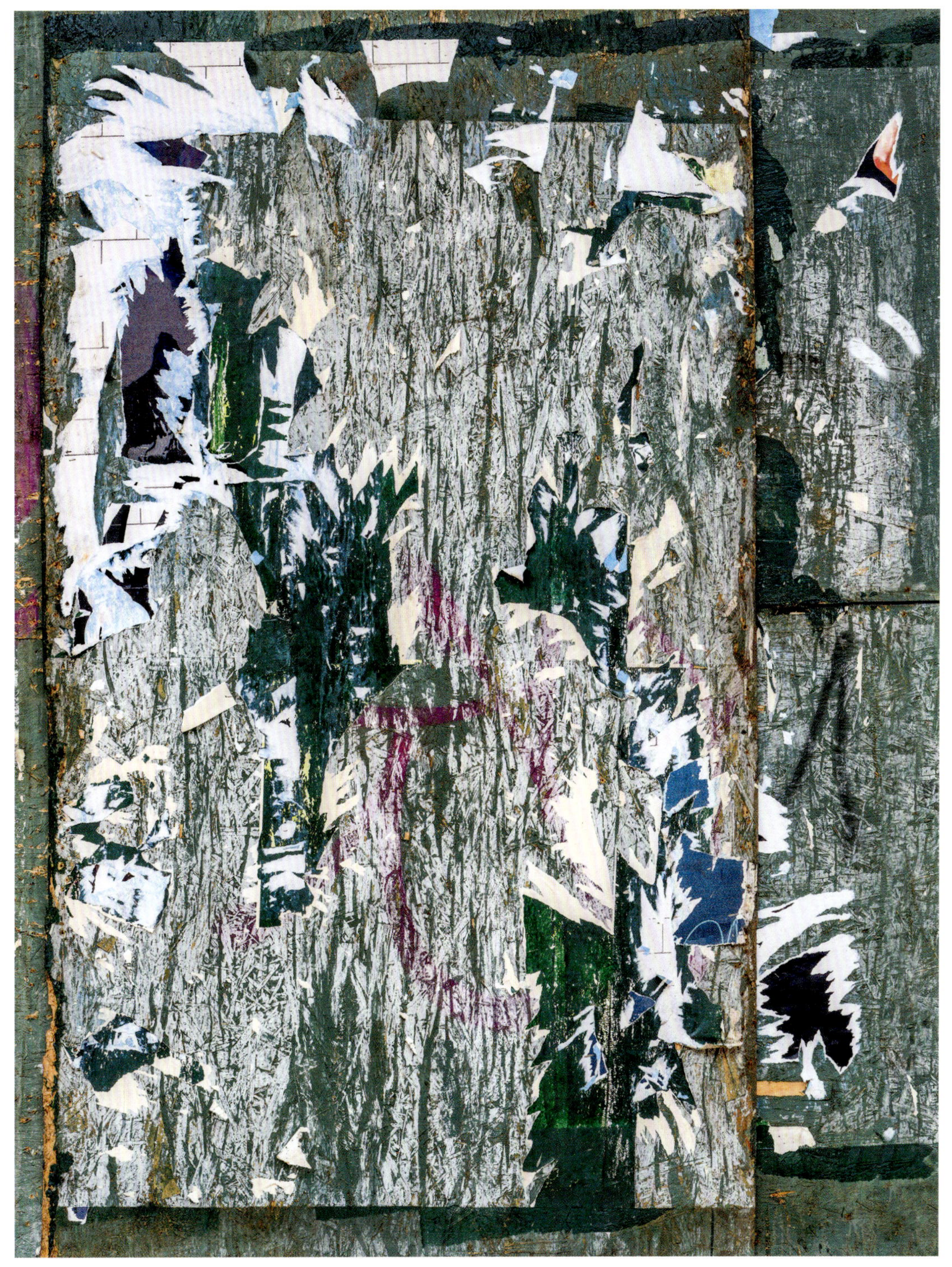

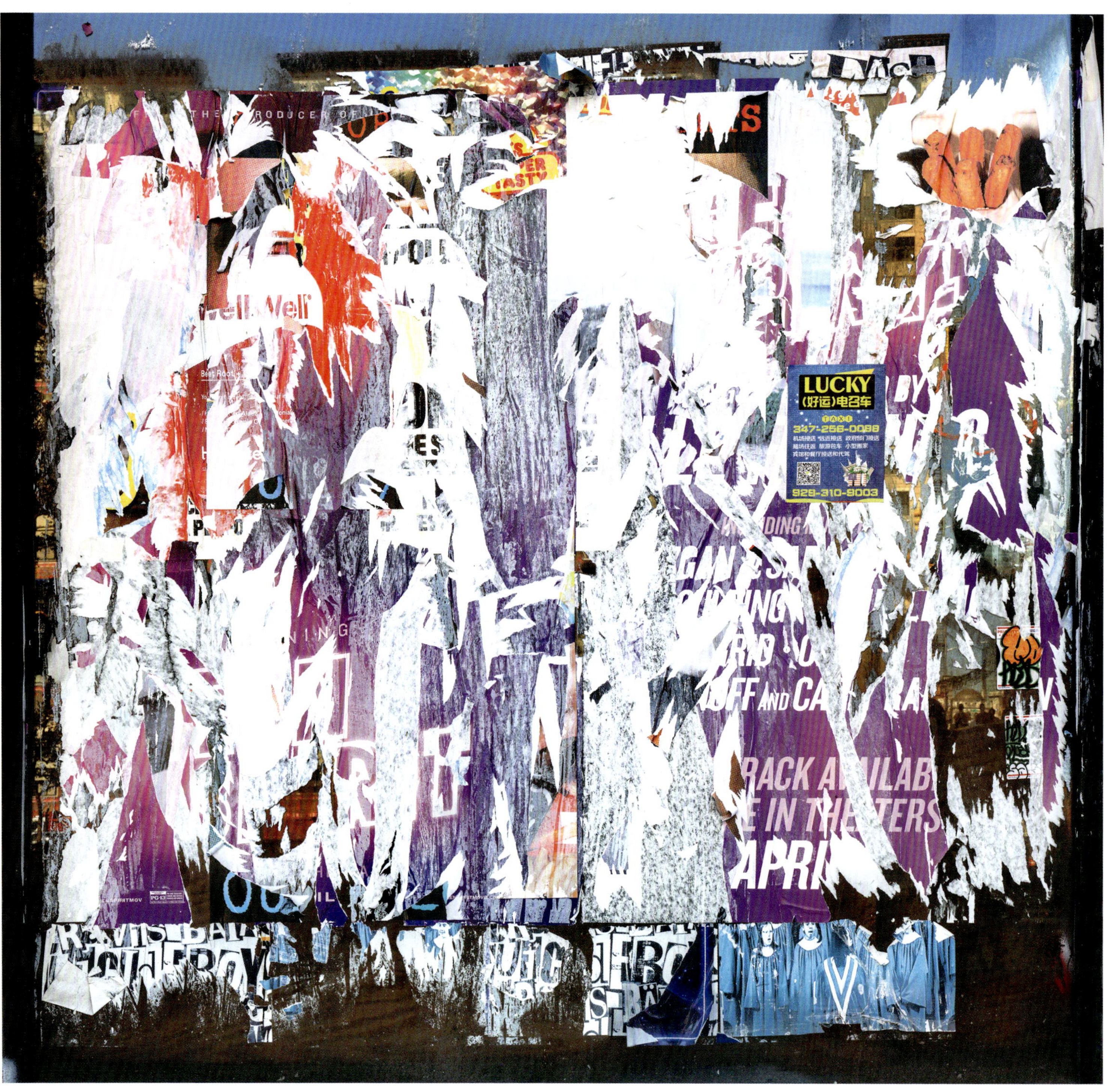
Well Well
LUCKY
〈好运〉电召车
347-256-0088
929-310-9003
RACK AVAILAB
E IN THEATERS
APRI

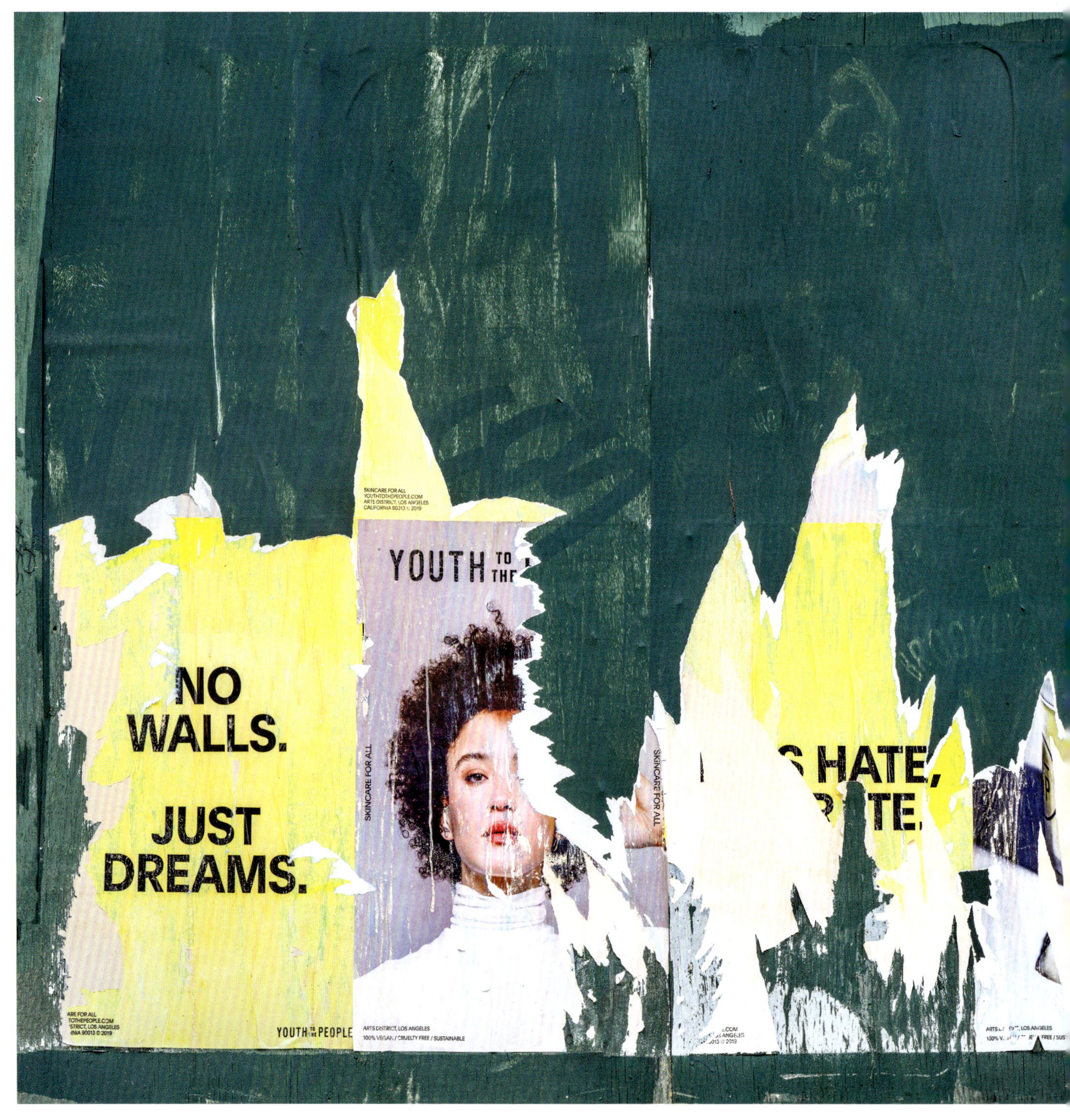
NO WALLS.

JUST DREAMS.

YOUTH TO THE PEOPLE

SKINCARE FOR ALL
YOUTHTOTHEPEOPLE.COM
ARTS DISTRICT, LOS ANGELES
CALIFORNIA 90213 © 2019

SKINCARE FOR ALL

SKINCARE FOR ALL

YOUTH TO THE PEOPLE

ARTS DISTRICT, LOS ANGELES
100% VEGAN / CRUELTY FREE / SUSTAINABLE

S HATE,
TE.

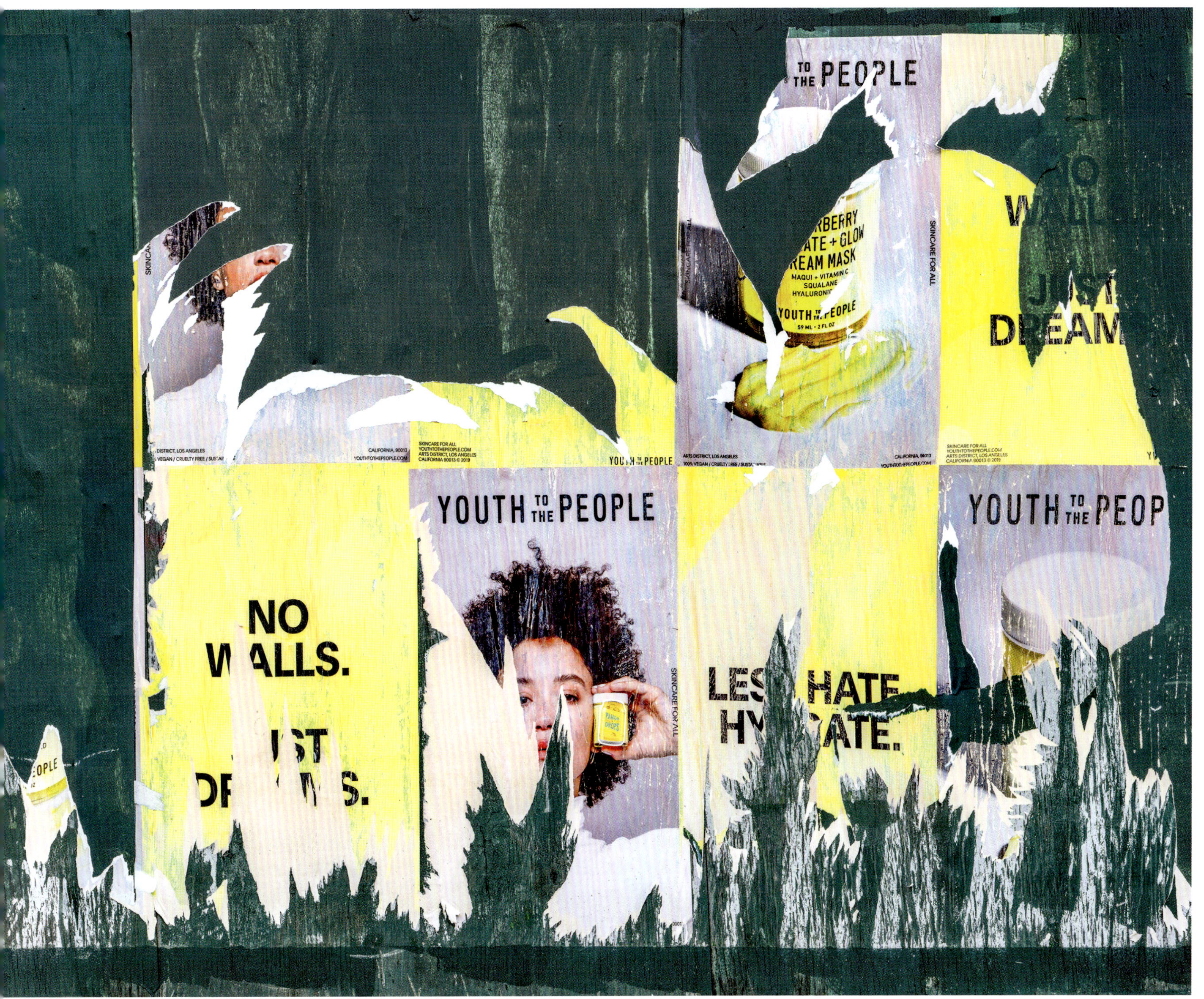

TO THE PEOPLE
RBERRY
ATE + GLOW
REAM MASK
MAQUI + VITAMIN C
SQUALANE
HYALURONIC
YOUTH TO THE PEOPLE
59 ML · 2 FL OZ
SKINCARE FOR ALL
NO
WALL
JUST
DREAM
YOUTH TO THE PEOPLE
NO
WALLS.
JUST
DREAMS.
LESS HATE.
HYDRATE.
YOUTH TO THE PEOPLE
YOUTH TO THE PEOP
SKINCARE FOR ALL

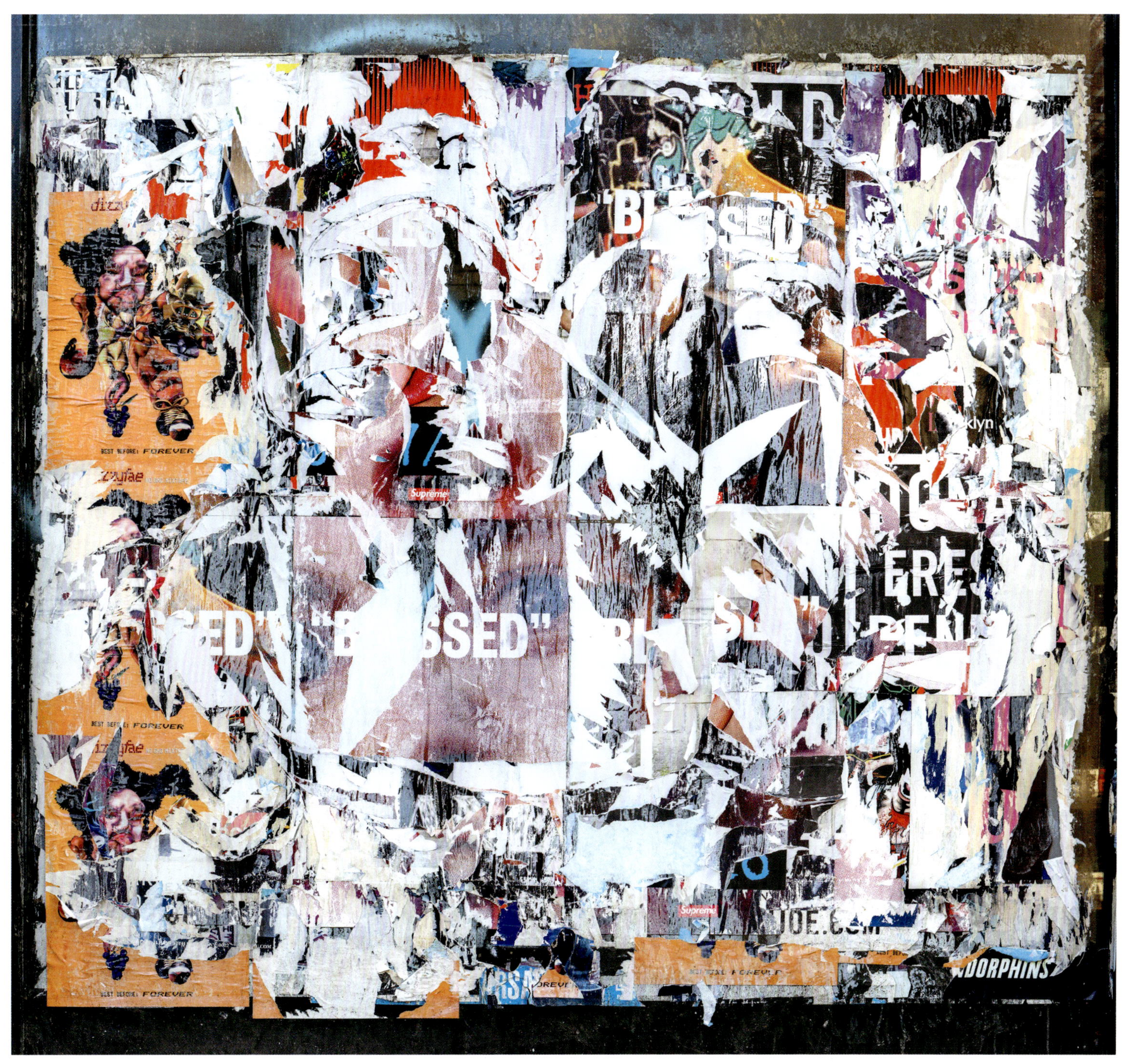

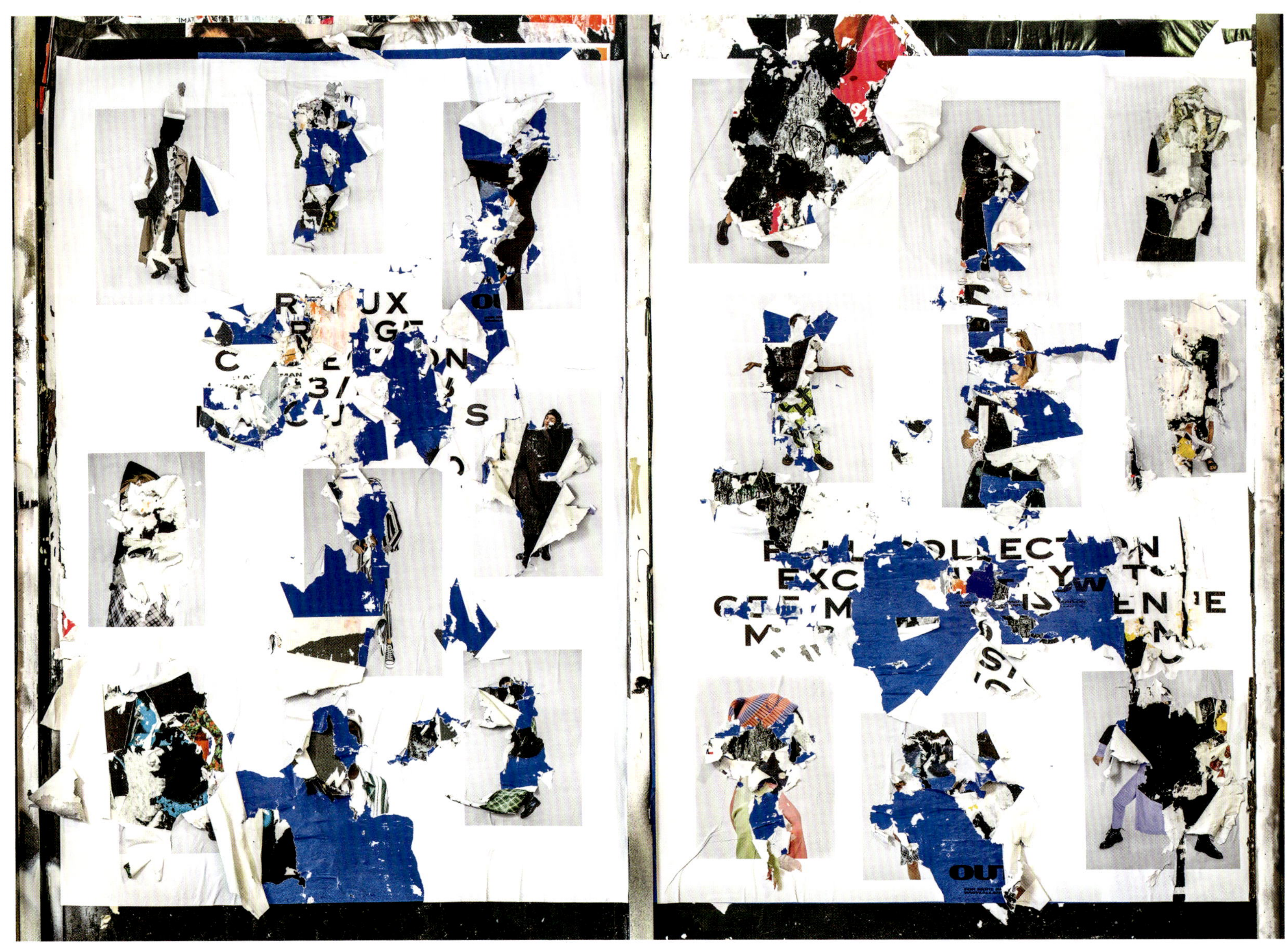

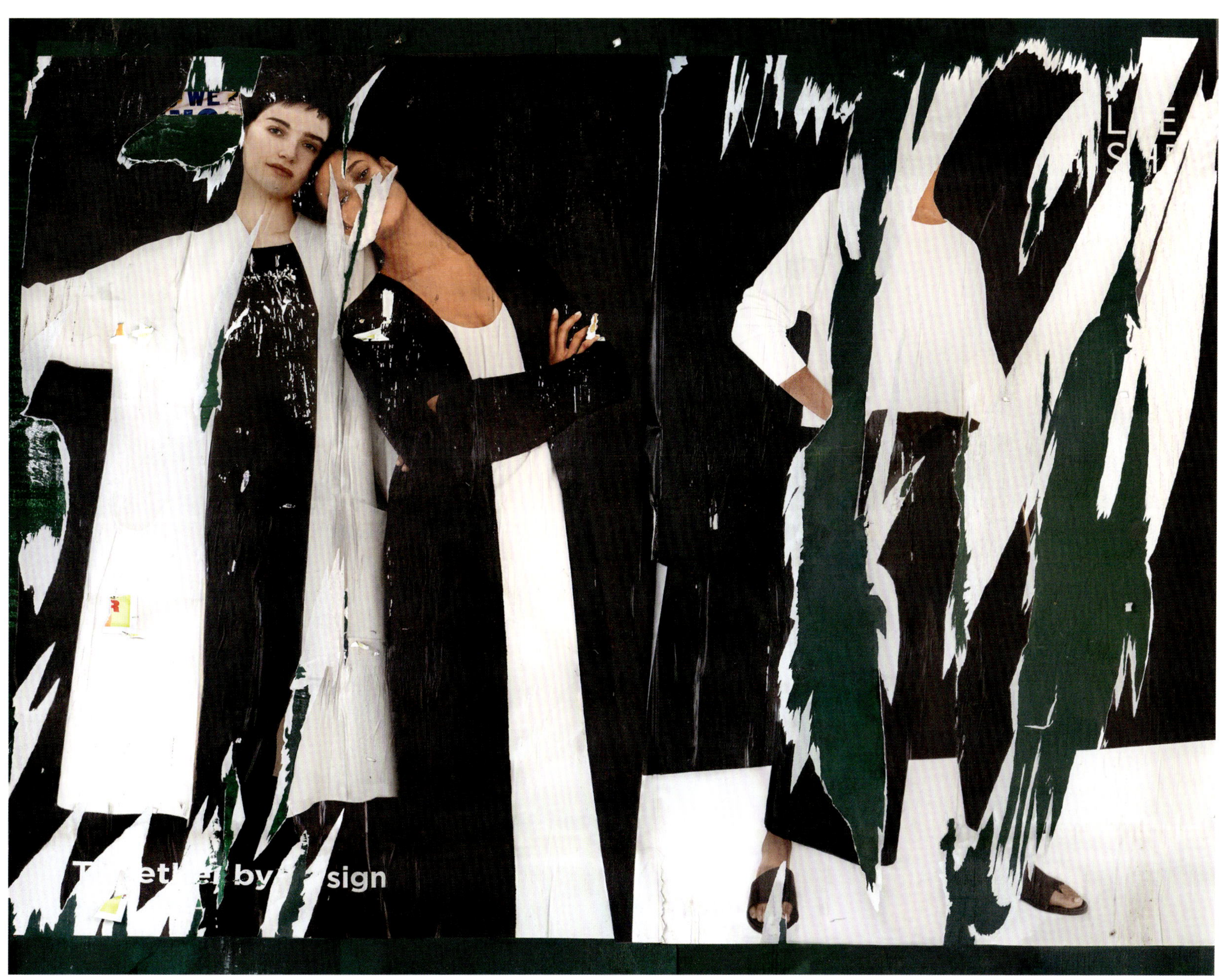
Together by design

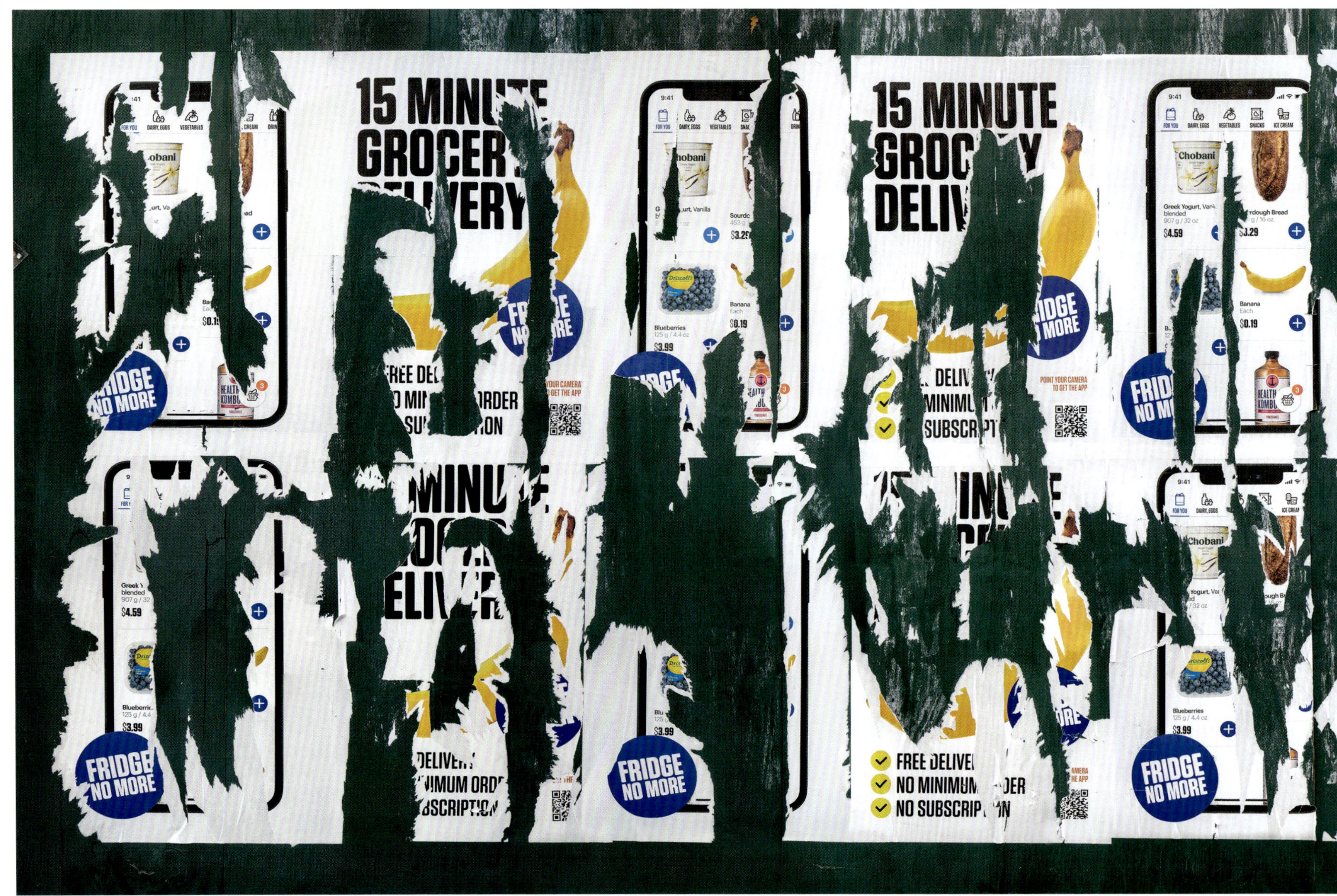
15 MINUTE
GROCERY
DELIVERY
FREE DELIVERY
NO MINIMUM ORDER
NO SUBSCRIPTION
FRIDGE
NO MORE
Chobani
Greek Yogurt, Vanilla
blended
907 g / 32 oz
$4.59
Sourdough Bread
16 oz
$3.29
Blueberries
125 g / 4.4 oz
$3.99
Banana
Each
$0.19
POINT YOUR CAMERA
TO GET THE APP
FOR YOU
DAIRY, EGGS
VEGETABLES
SNACKS
ICE CREAM
9:41
HEALTHY KOMBUCHA

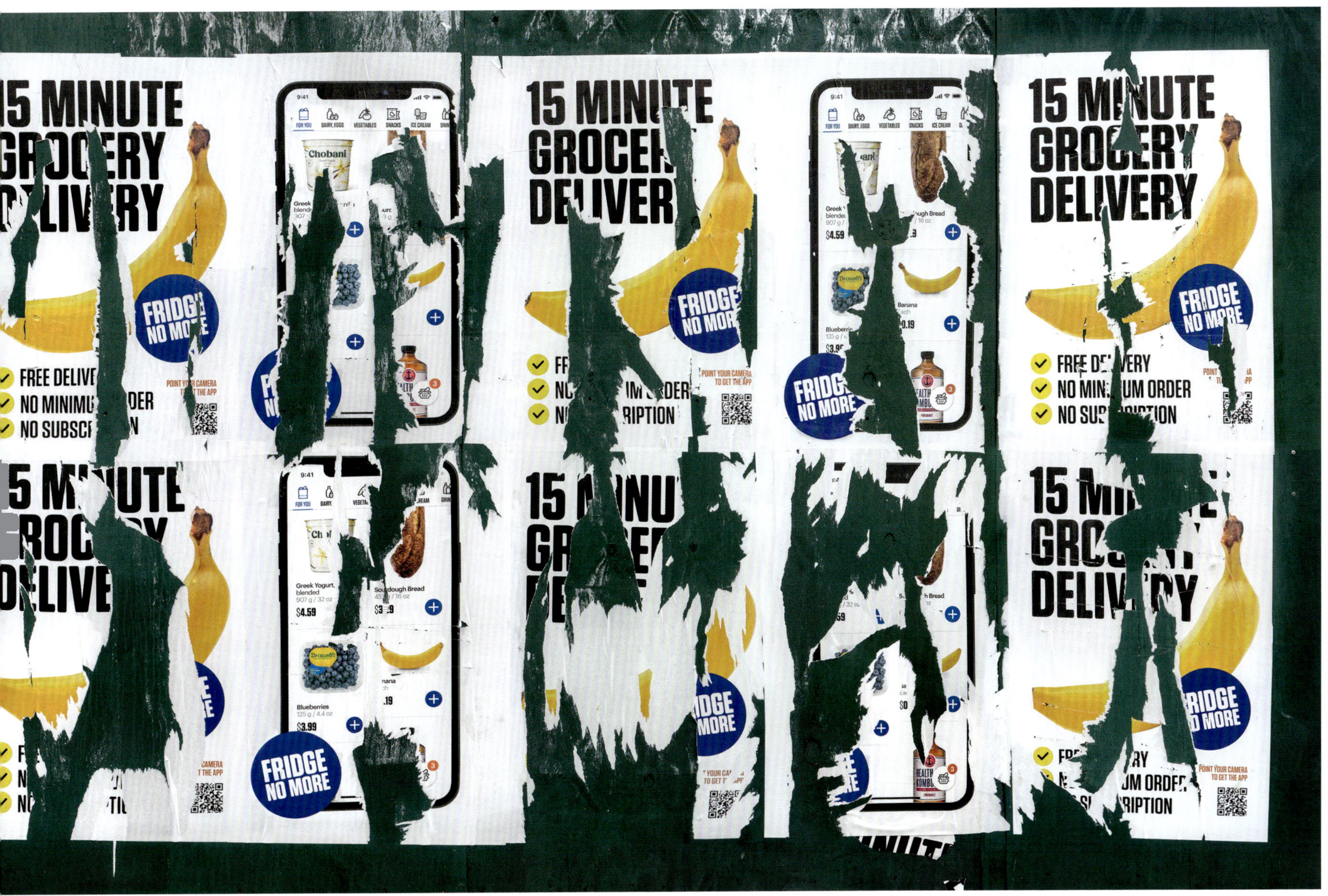
15 MINUTE GROCERY DELIVERY
FRIDGE NO MORE
FREE DELIVERY
NO MINIMUM ORDER
NO SUBSCRIPTION
POINT YOUR CAMERA TO GET THE APP
9:41
FOR YOU
DAIRY, EGGS
VEGETABLES
SNACKS
ICE CREAM
Chobani
Greek Yogurt, blended
907 g / 32 oz
$4.59
Sourdough Bread
453 g / 16 oz
$3.99
Blueberries
125 g / 4.4 oz
$3.99
Banana
each
$0.19

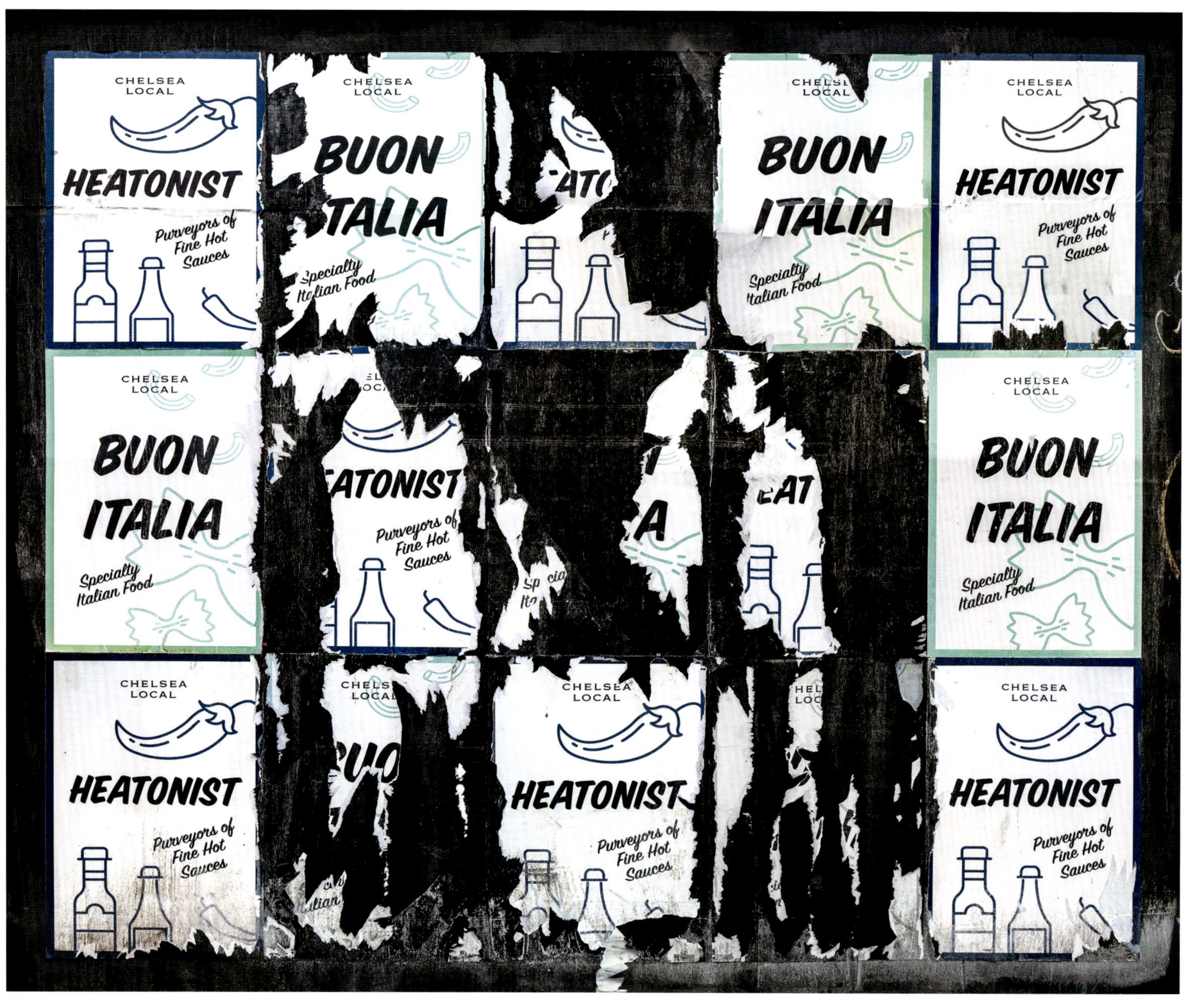
CHELSEA LOCAL
HEATONIST
Purveyors of Fine Hot Sauces
CHELSEA LOCAL
BUON ITALIA
Specialty Italian Food
BUON ITALIA
Specialty Italian Food
CHELSEA LOCAL
HEATONIST
Purveyors of Fine Hot Sauces
CHELSEA LOCAL
BUON ITALIA
Specialty Italian Food
HEATONIST
Purveyors of Fine Hot Sauces
BUON ITALIA
Specialty Italian Food
CHELSEA LOCAL
HEATONIST
Purveyors of Fine Hot Sauces
CHELSEA LOCAL
HEATONIST
Purveyors of Fine Hot Sauces
CHELSEA LOCAL
HEATONIST
Purveyors of Fine Hot Sauces

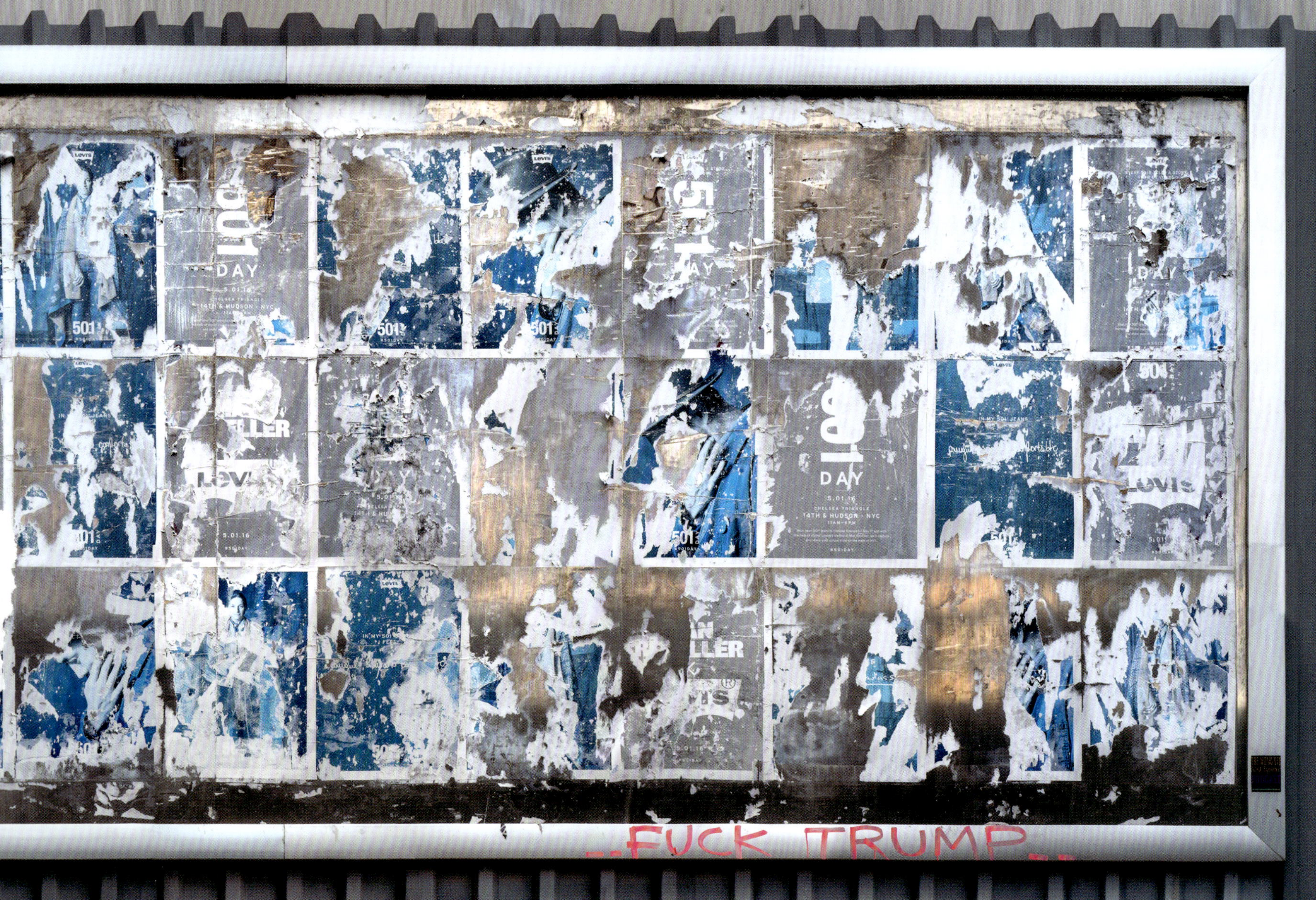
501
DAY
5.01.16
CHELSEA TRIANGLE
14TH & HUDSON - NYC
501
DAY
FUCK TRUMP

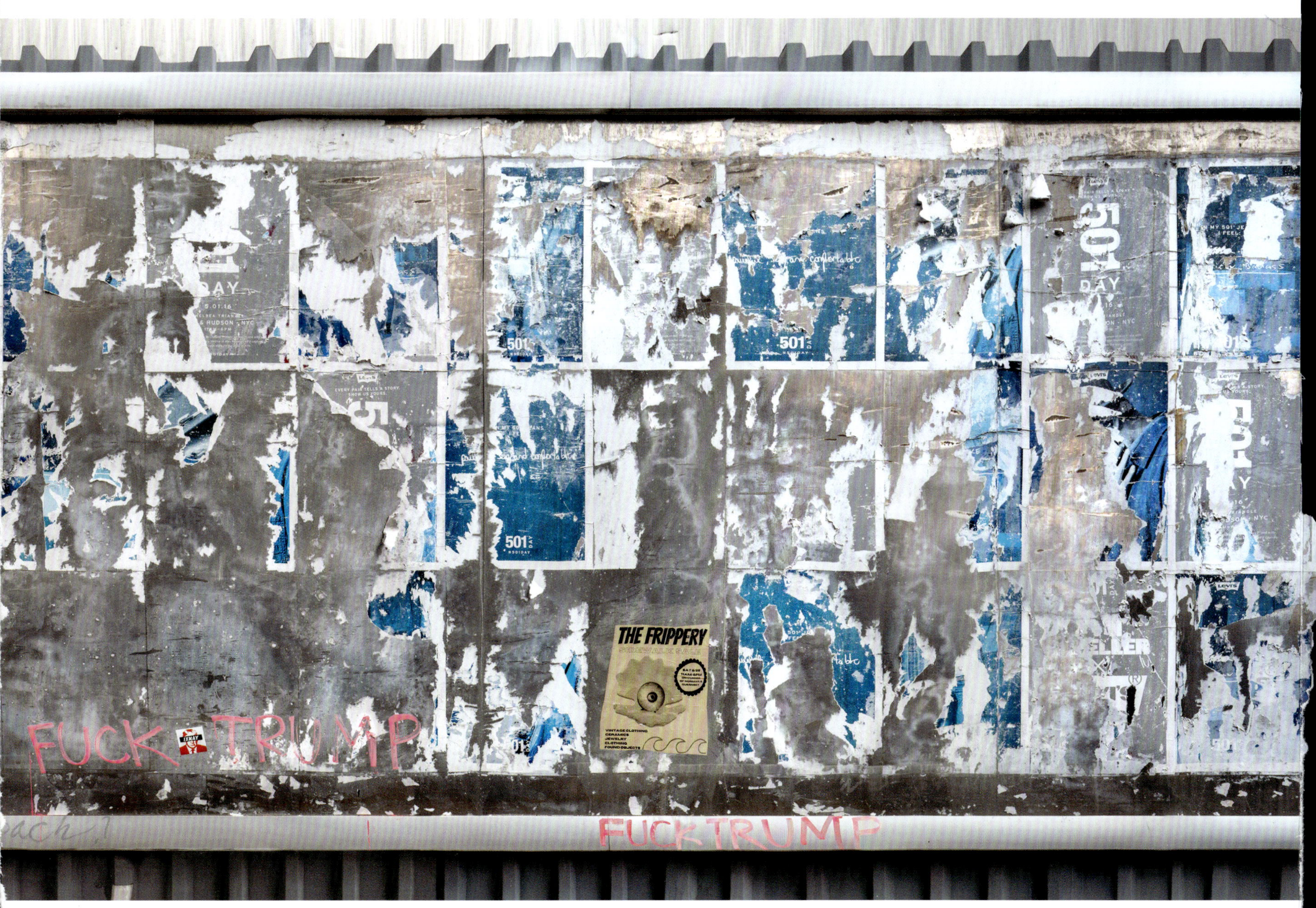

FUCK TRUMP
FUCKTRUMP
THE FRIPPERY
501
DAY

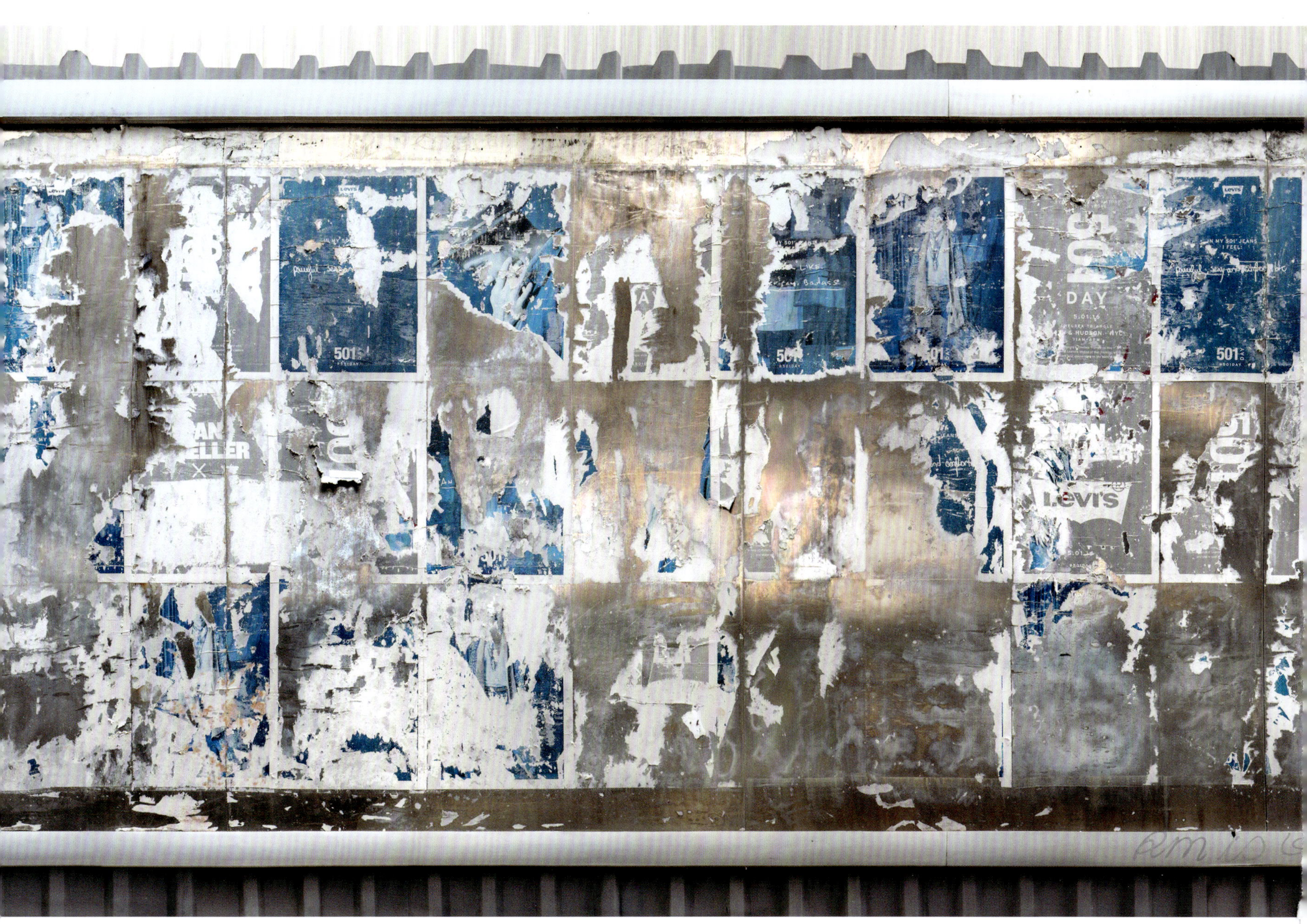
501
DAY
5.01.16
501
LEVI'S

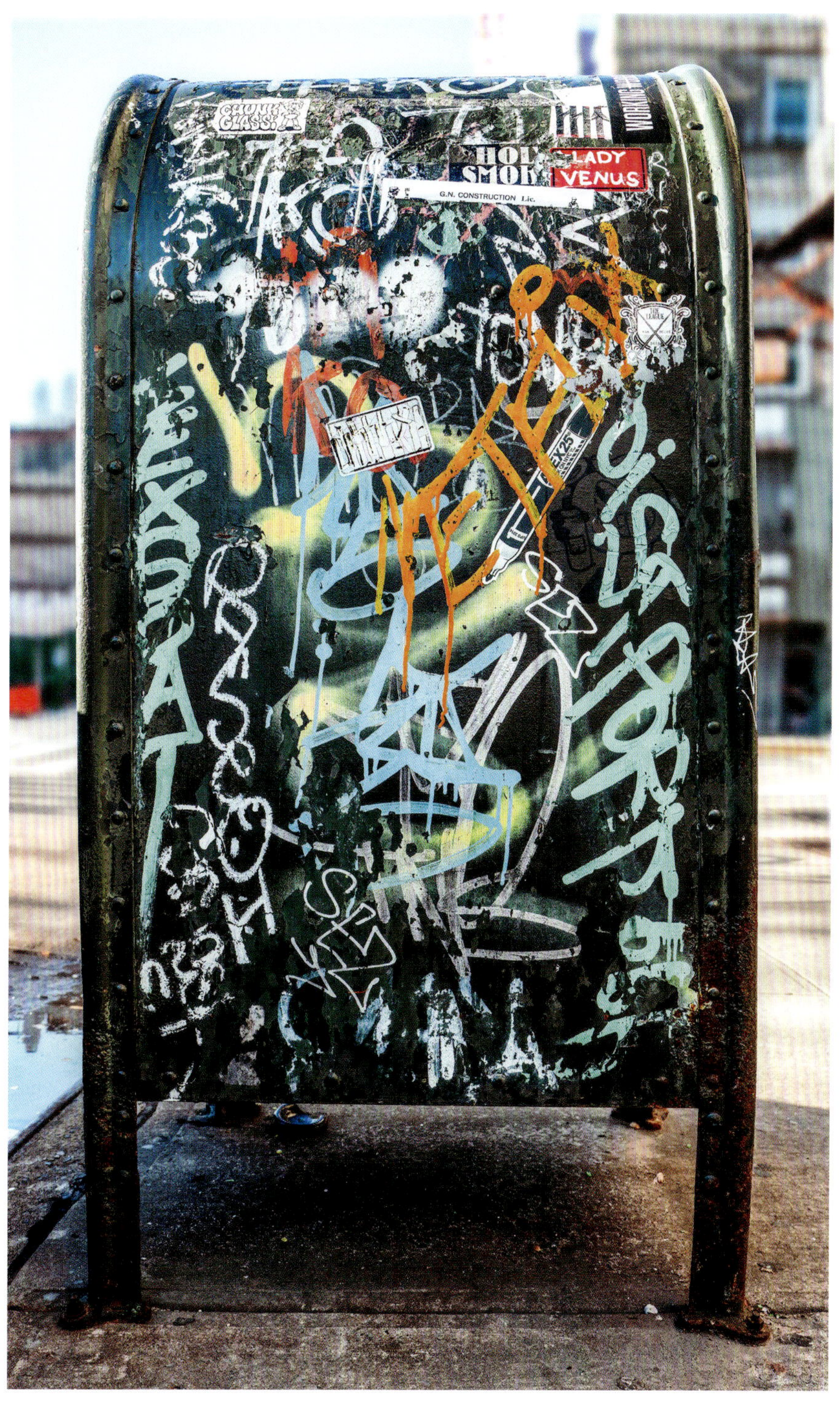

CHUNK CLASSIX
HOT SMOK
LADY VENUS
WORK
G.N. CONSTRUCTION Lic.

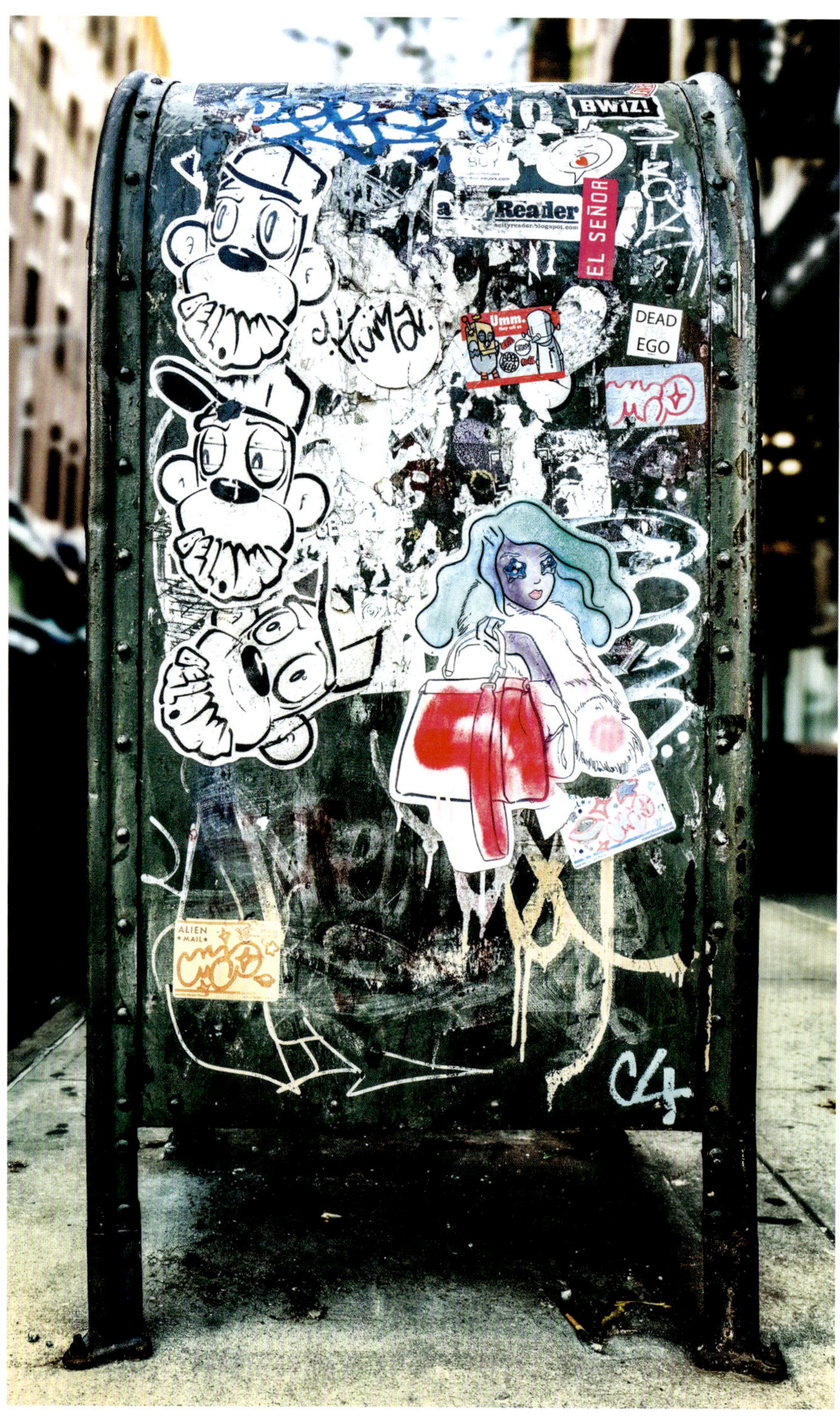
BWiZ!
Reader
EL SEÑOR
Umm.
DEAD
EGO
ALIEN
MAIL

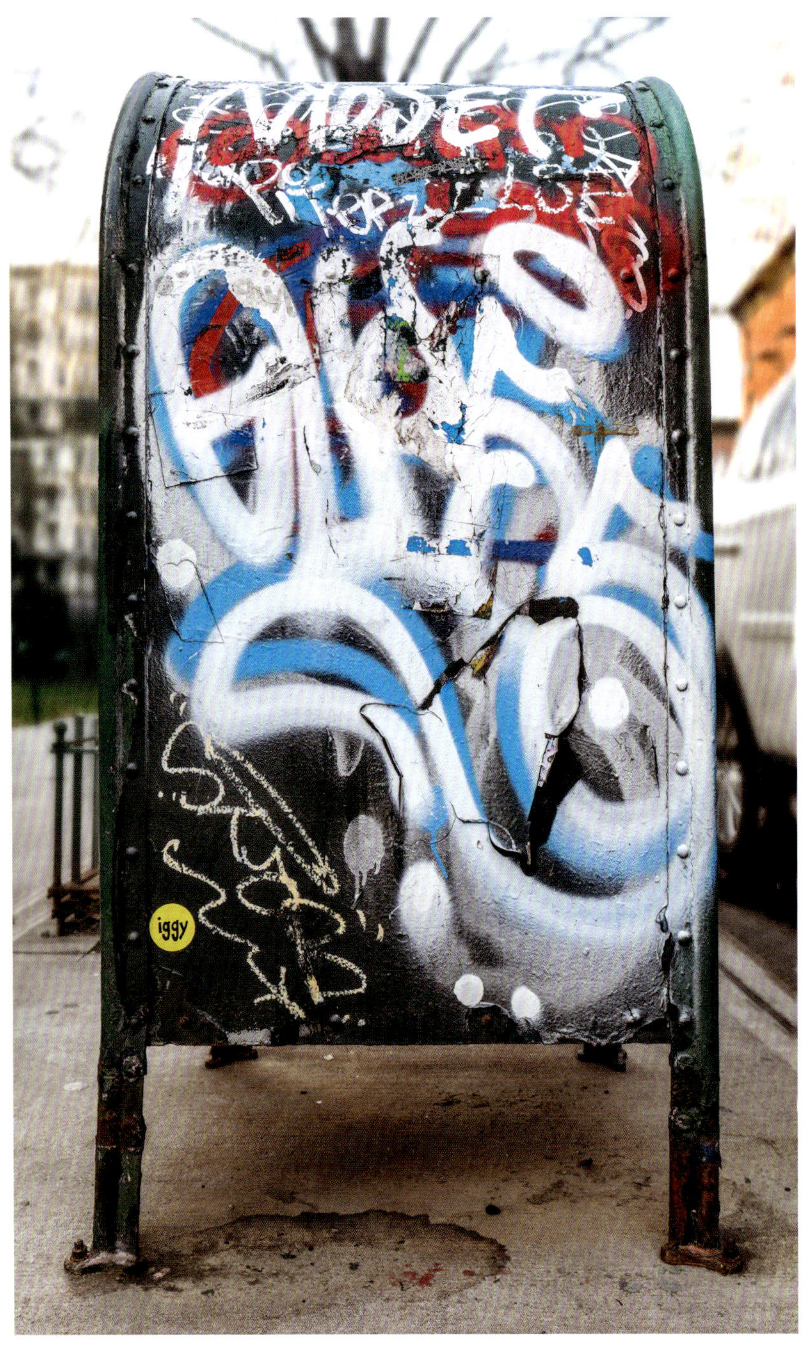
iggy

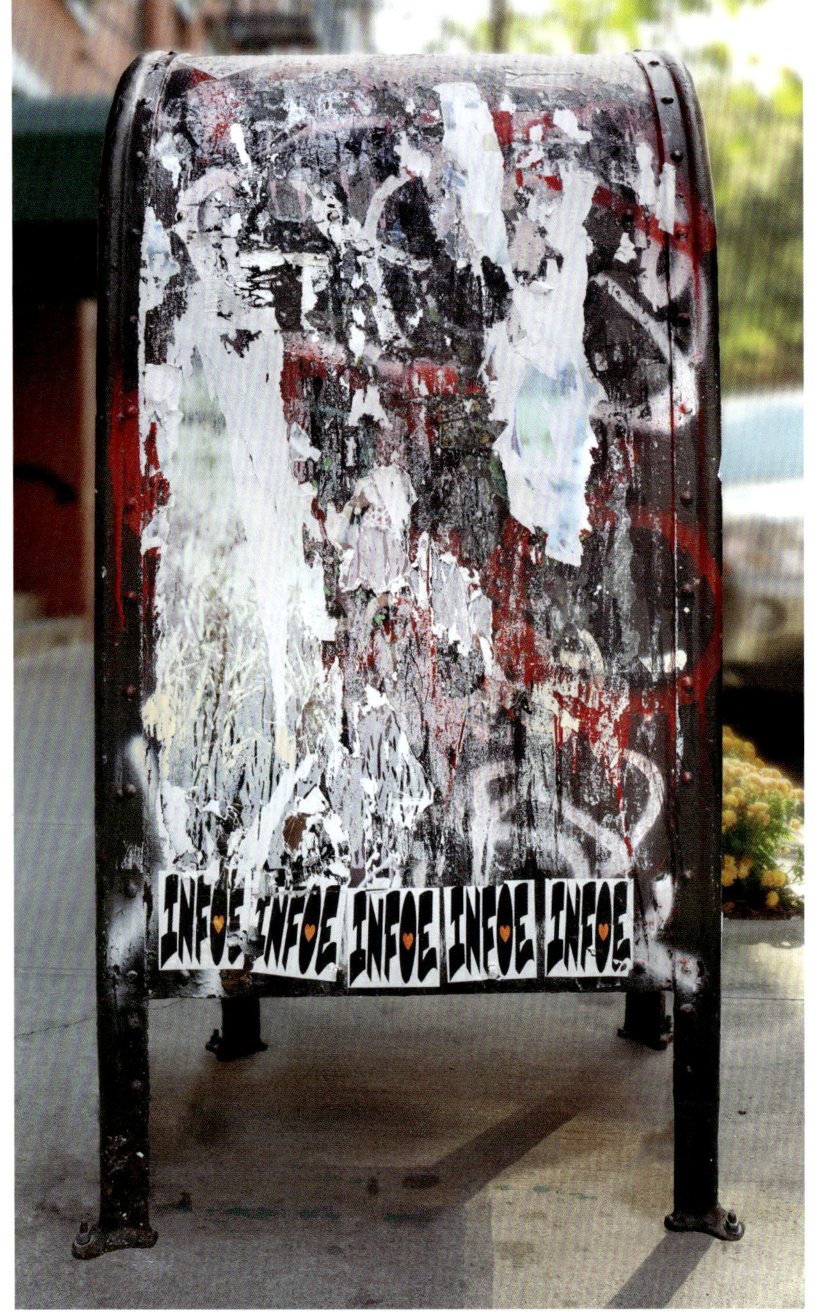
INFOE INFOE INFOE INFOE INFOE

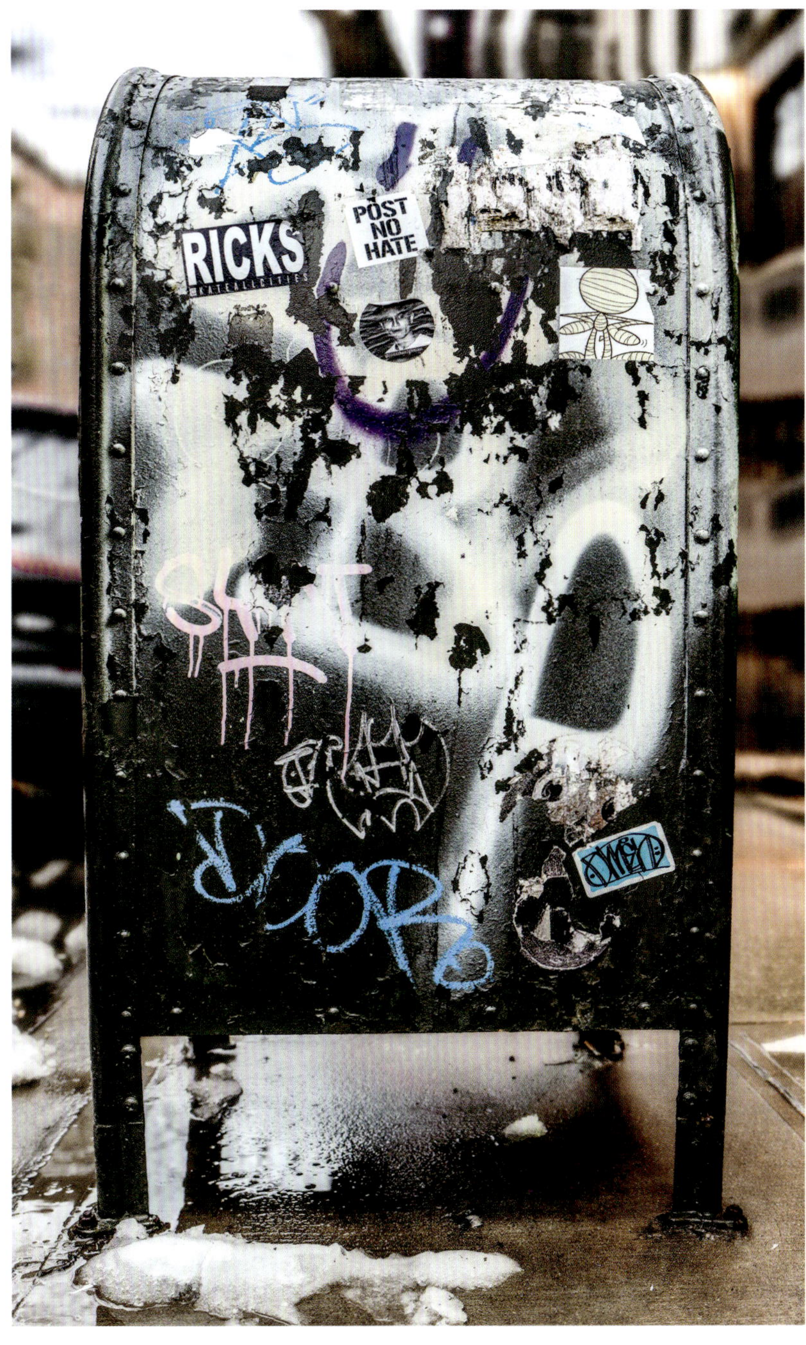
RICKS
POST
NO
HATE

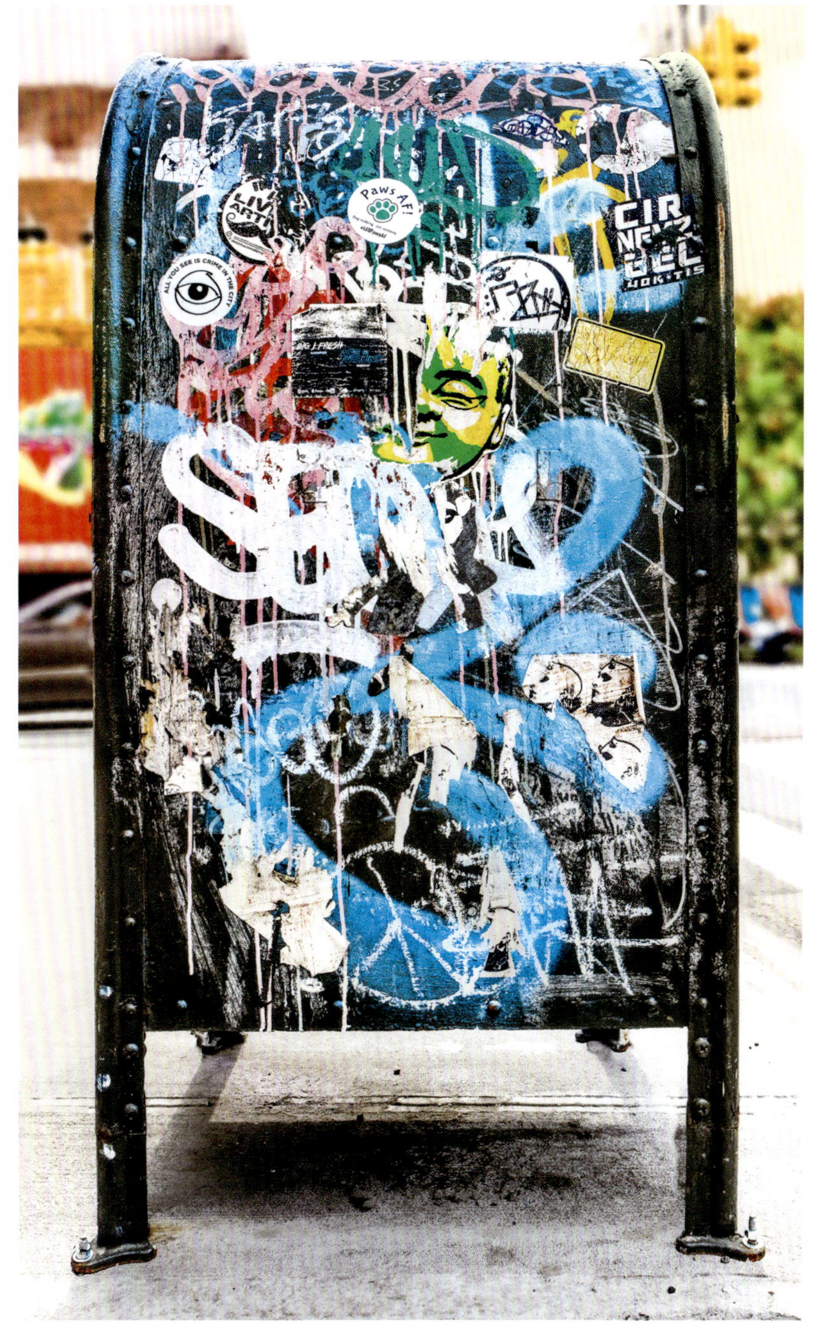
Paws AF!
CIR
NEW
BEL

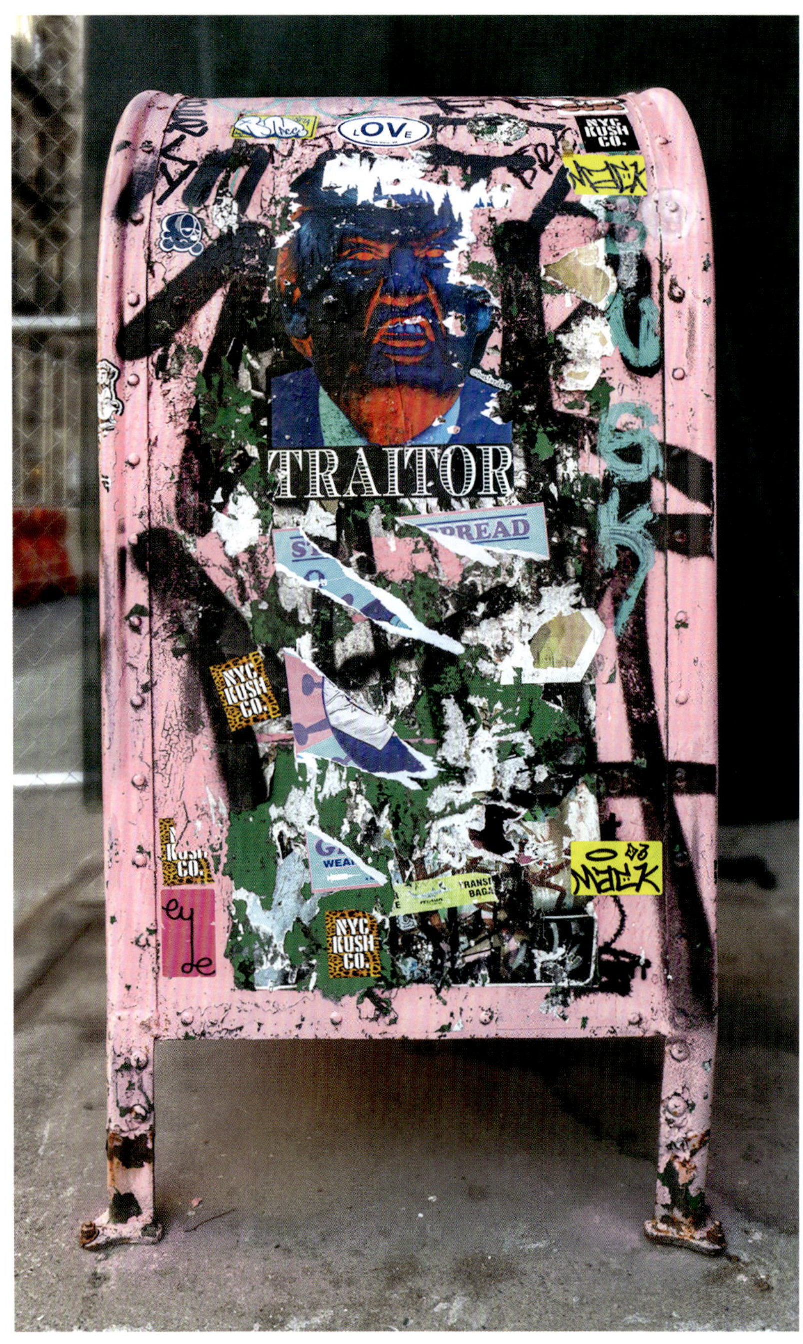
TRAITOR

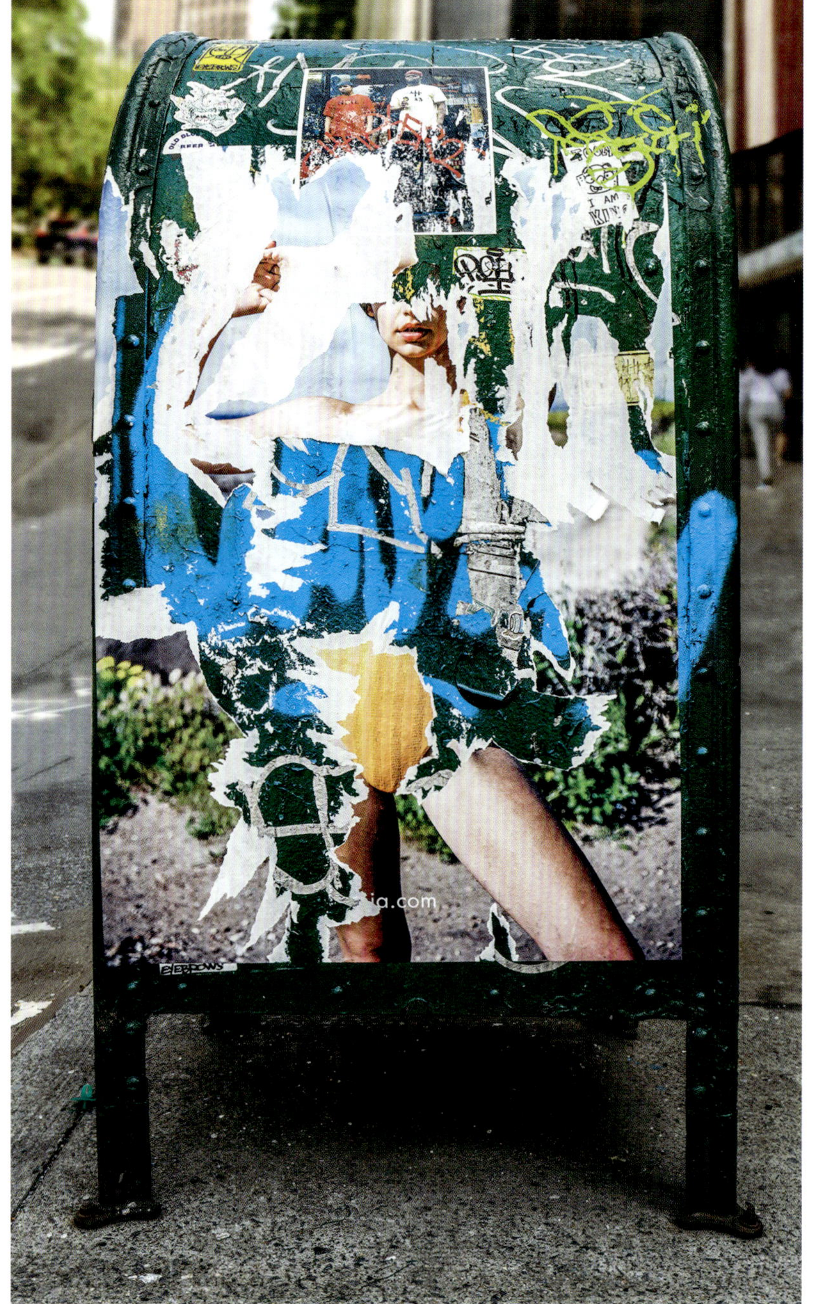

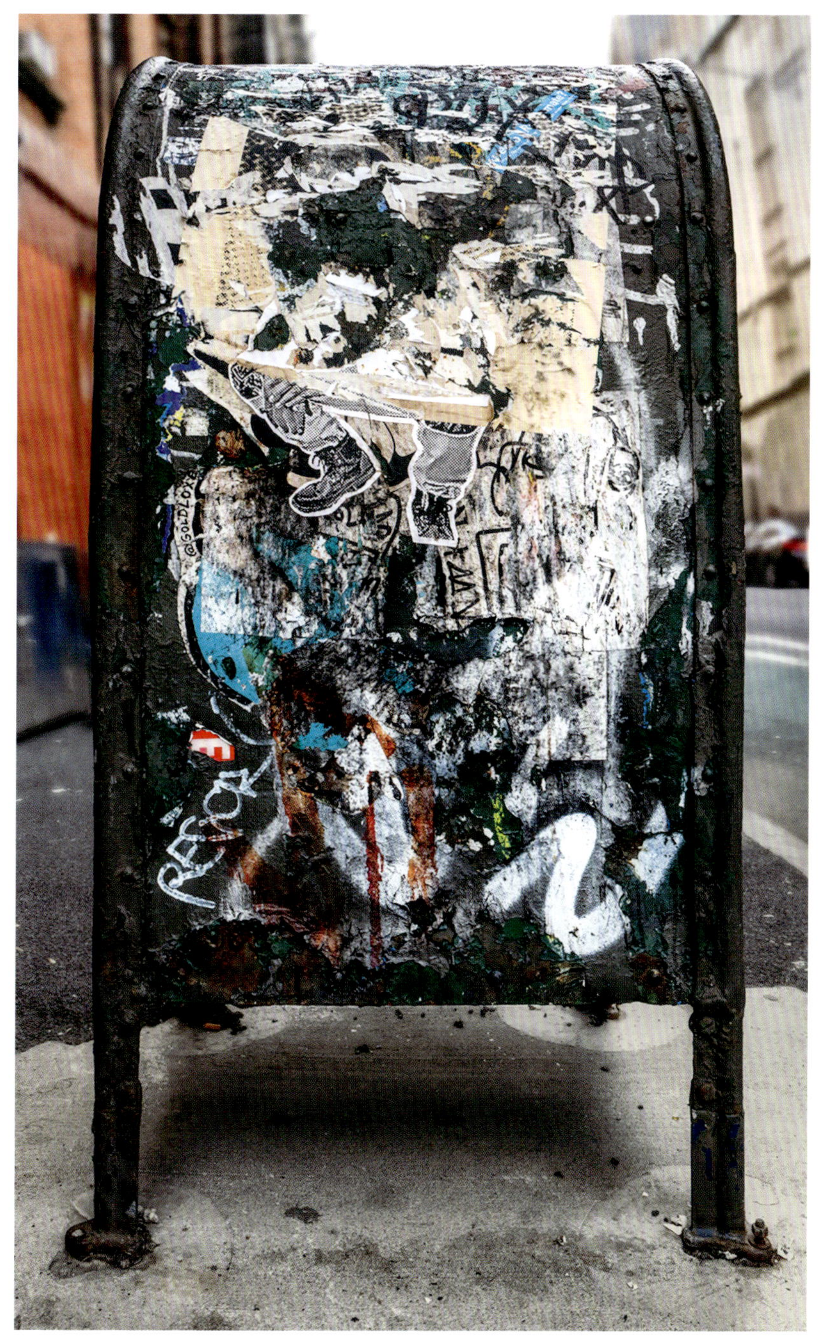
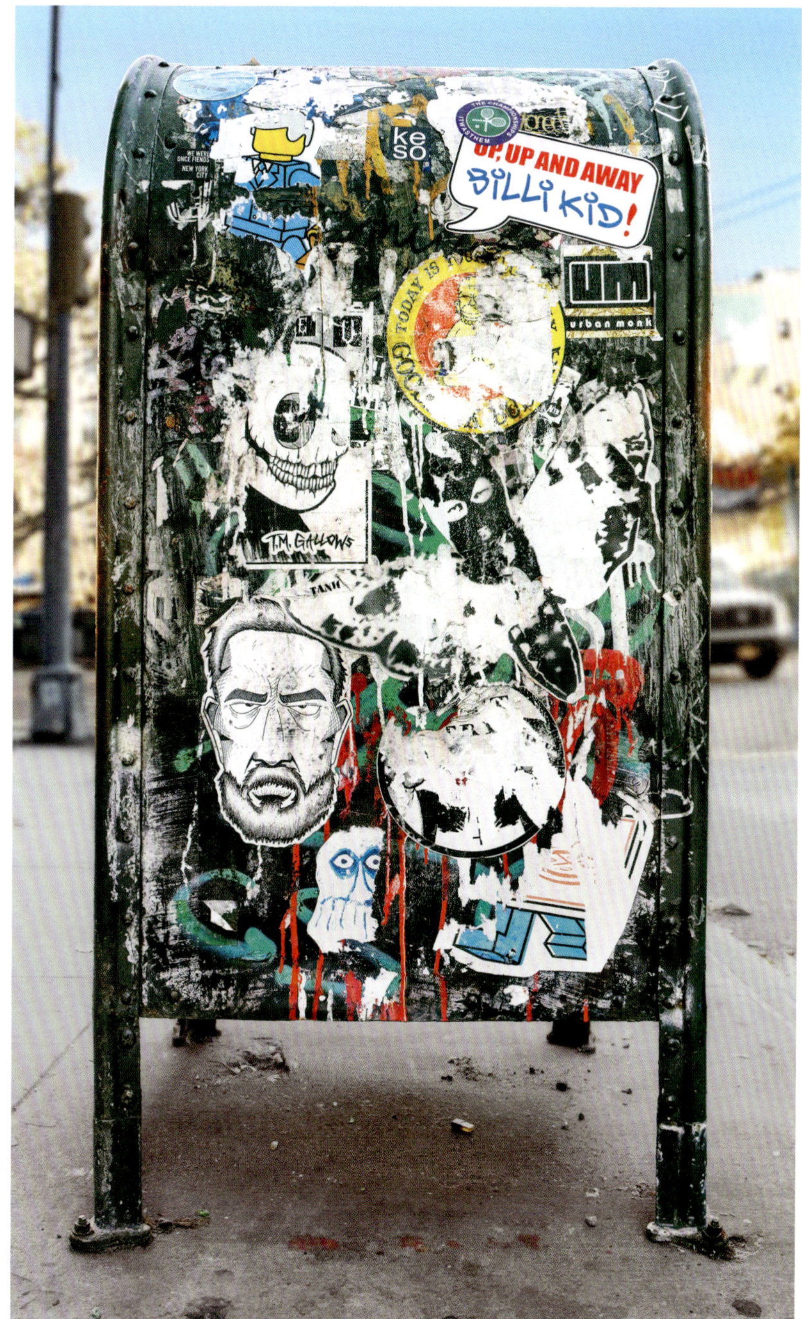
UP, UP AND AWAY
BiLLi KiD !
ke
so
UM
urban monk
T.M. GALLOWS

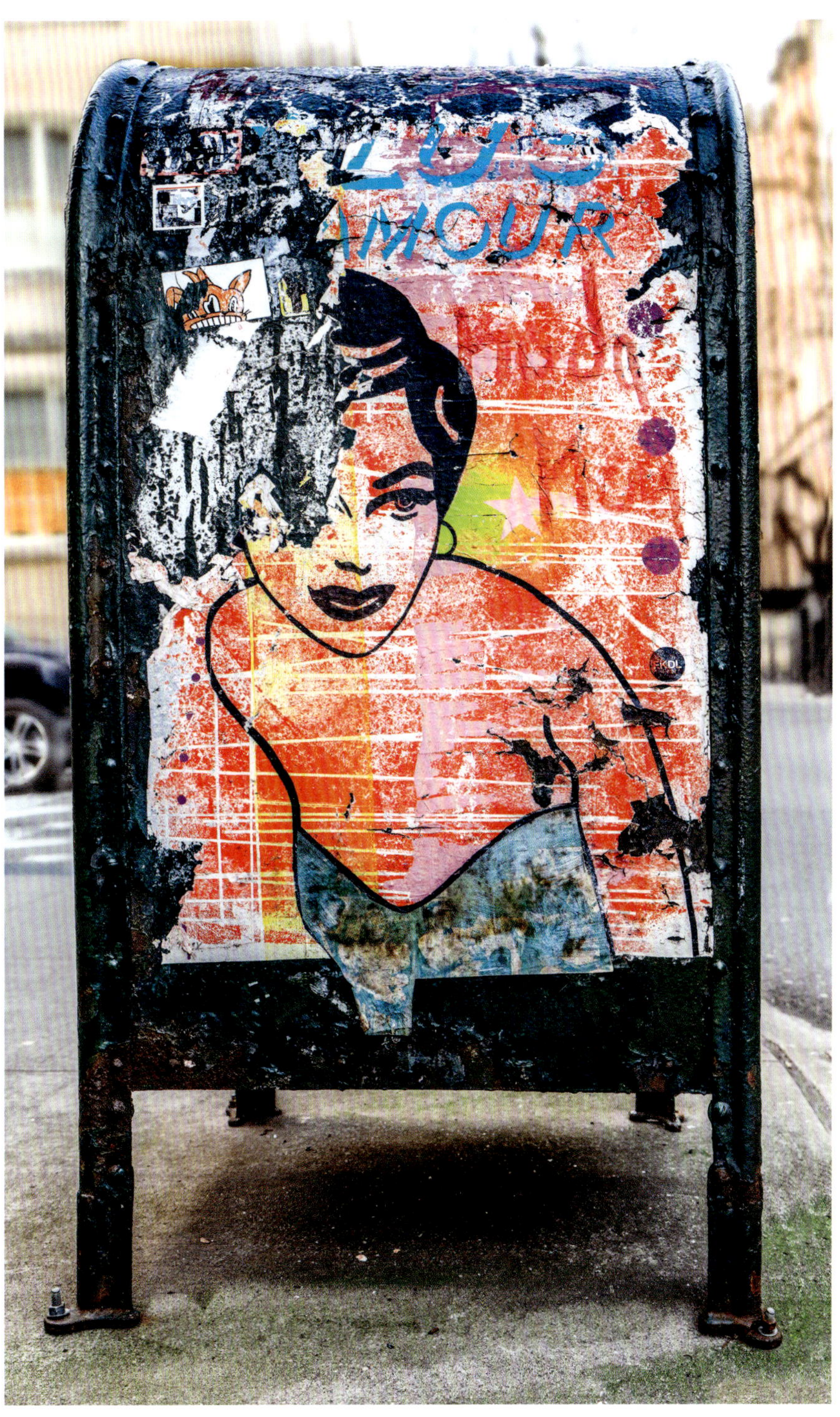
AMOUR

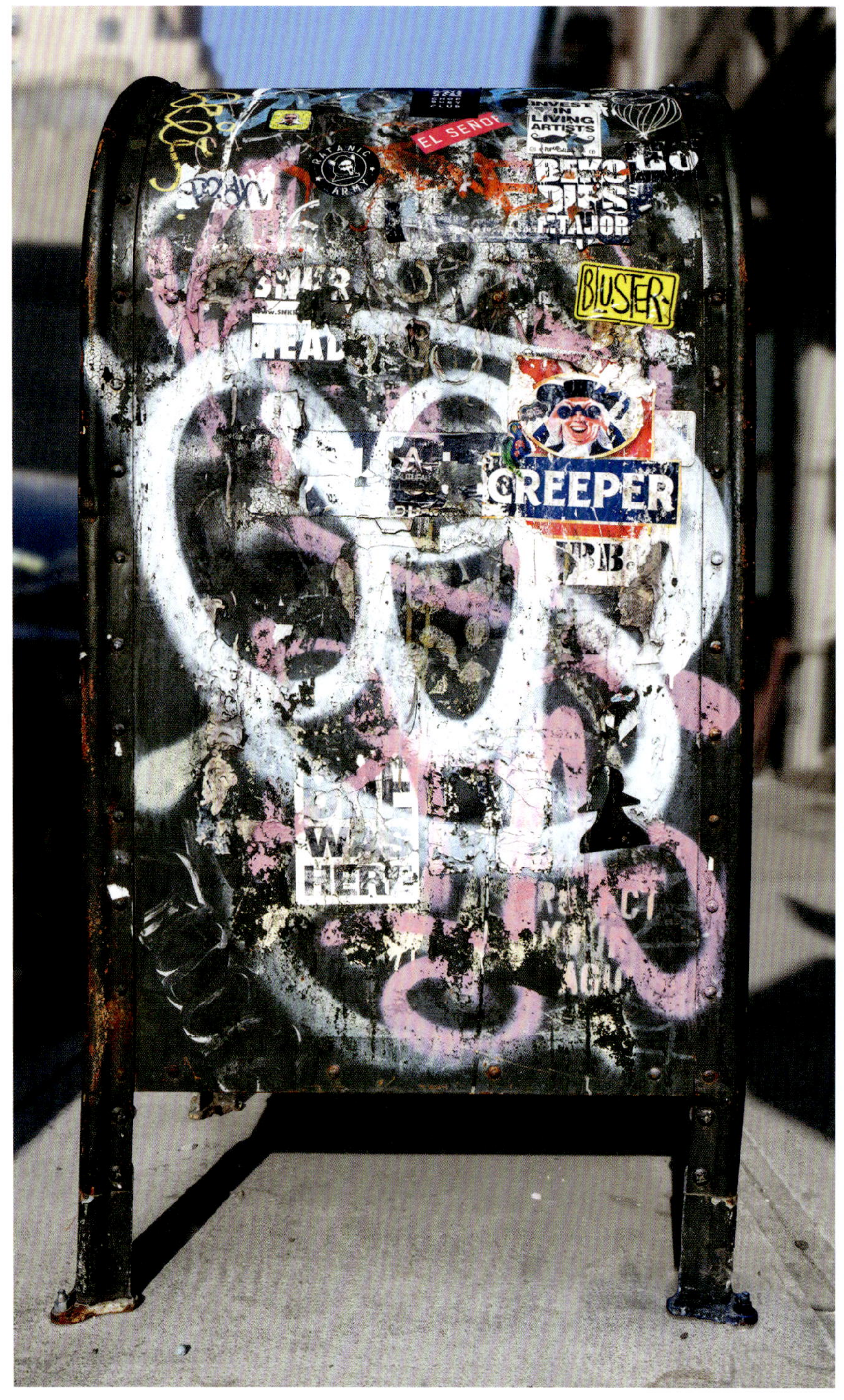
EL SEÑOR
SATANIC ARMY
INVEST IN LIVING ARTISTS
DIES
ETAJOR
BLUSTER
CREEPER
WAS HERE

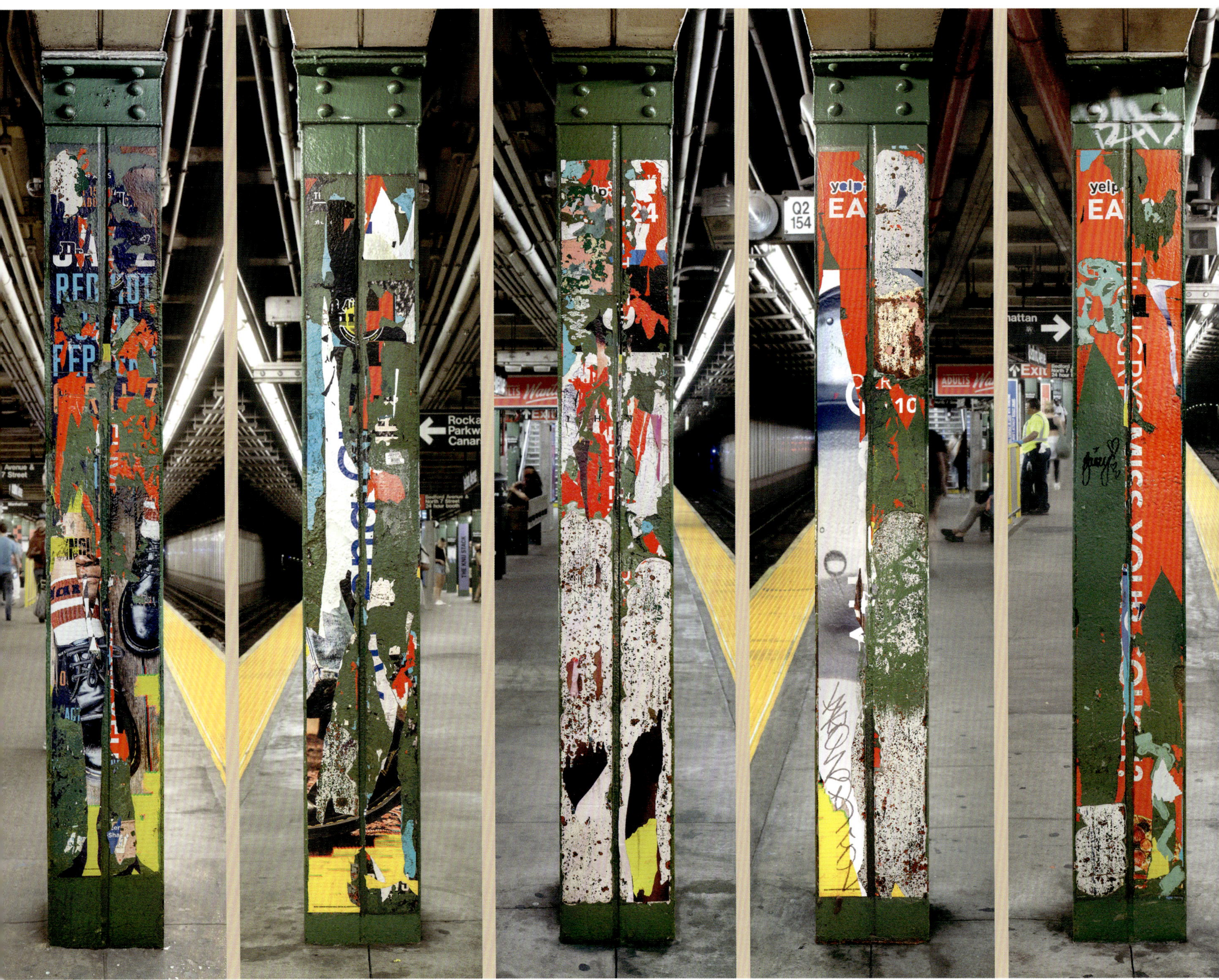

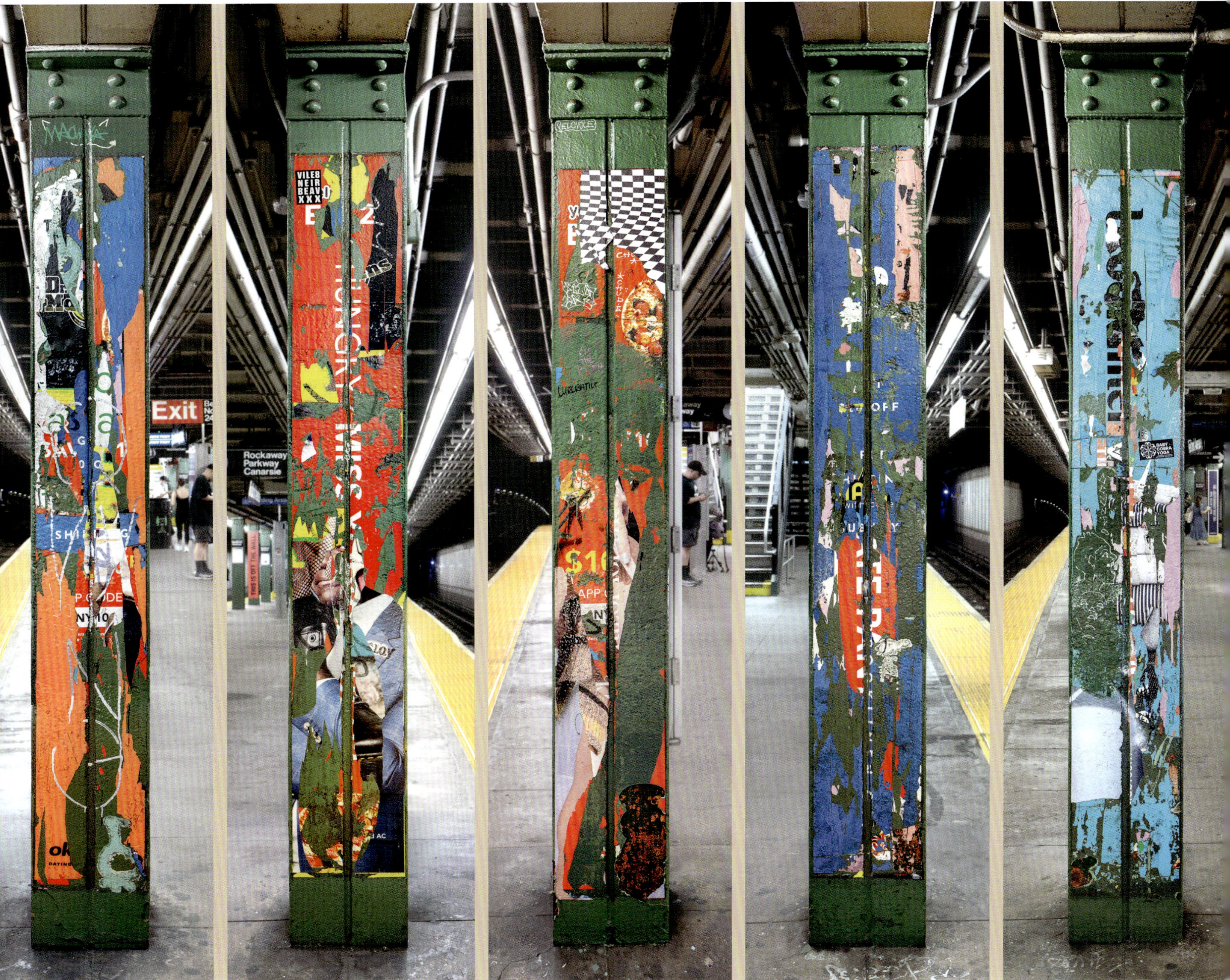

wall cuts

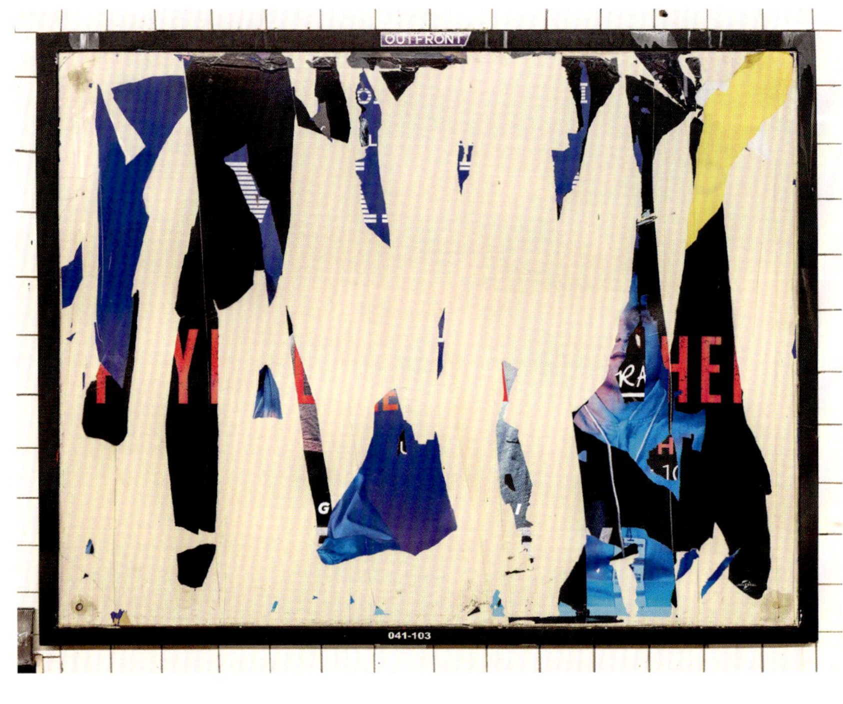

OUTFRONT
041-103

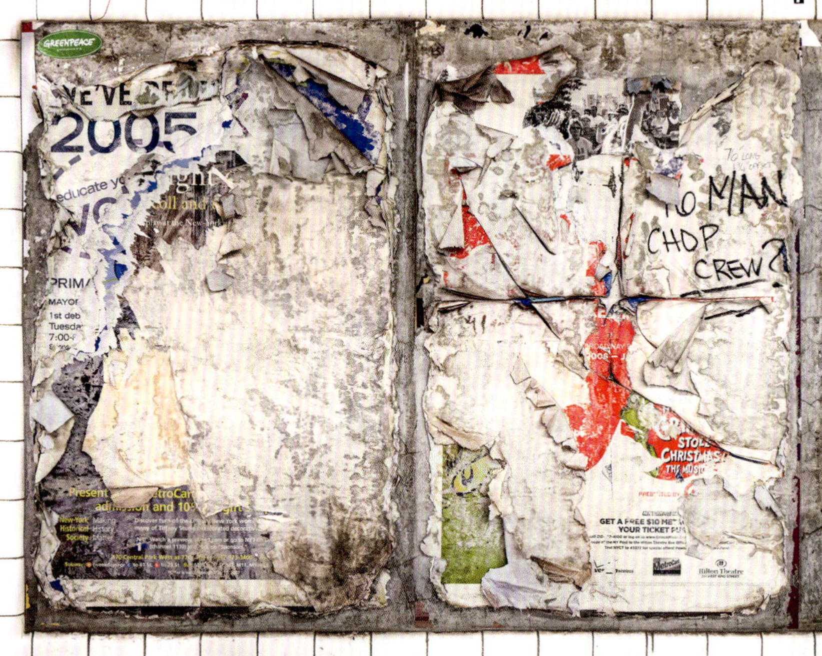

GREENPEACE
WE'VE
2005
educate yo
PRIMA
MAYOr
1st deb
Tuesda
7:00
NO MAN
CHOP
CREW?

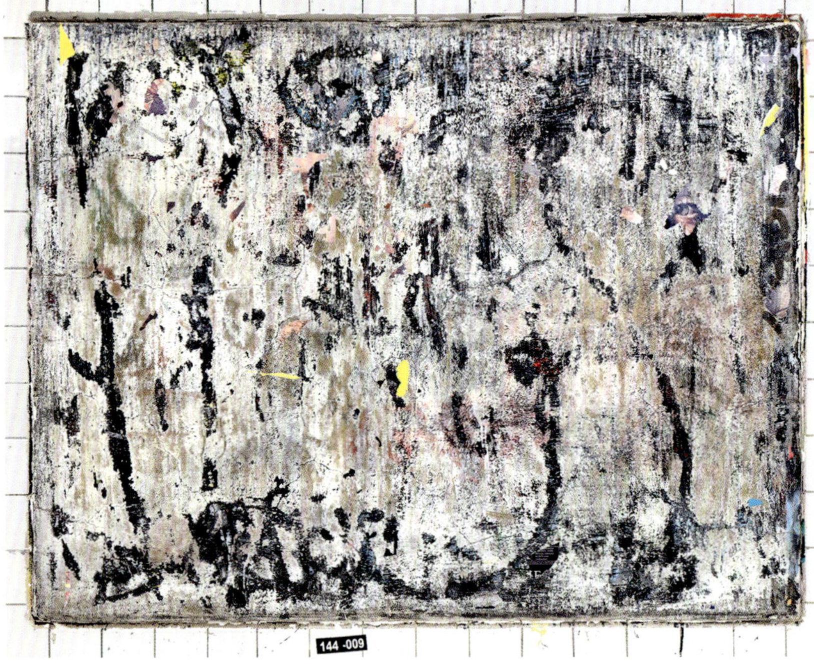

144 -009

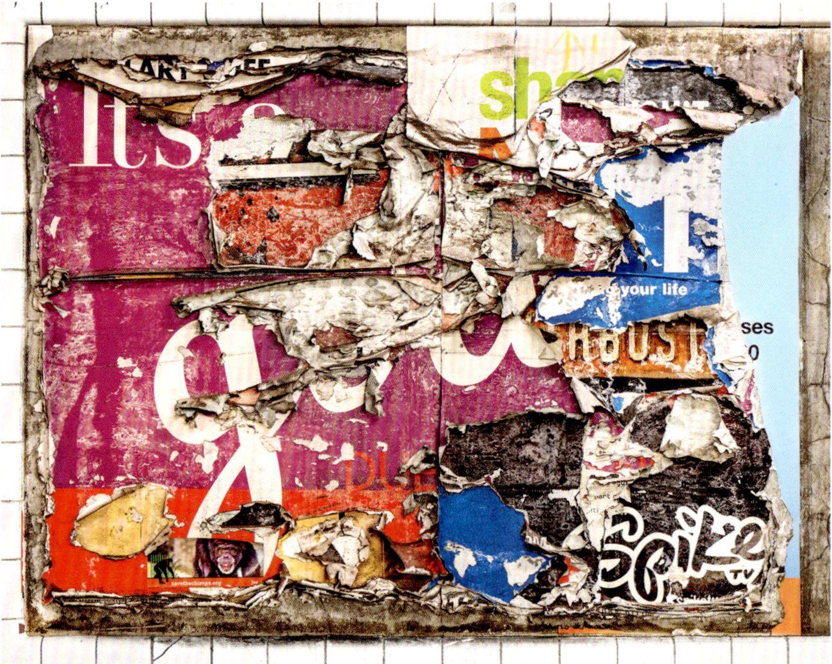

shop
Its
your life
ses

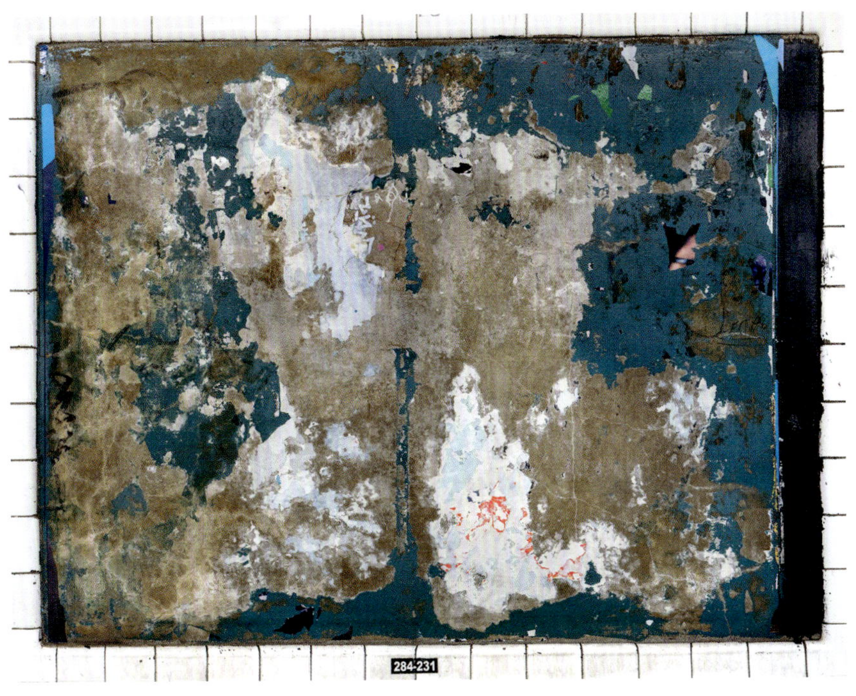

284-231

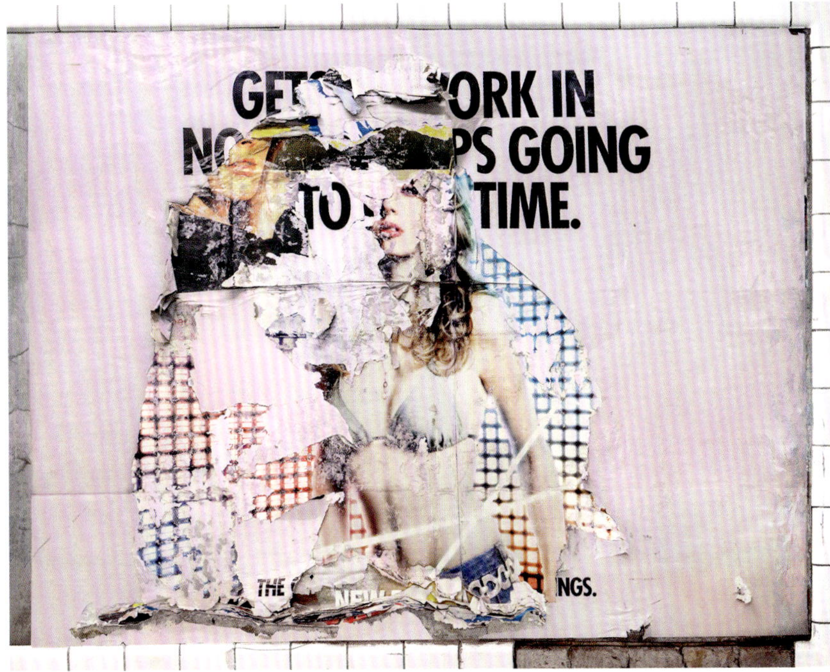

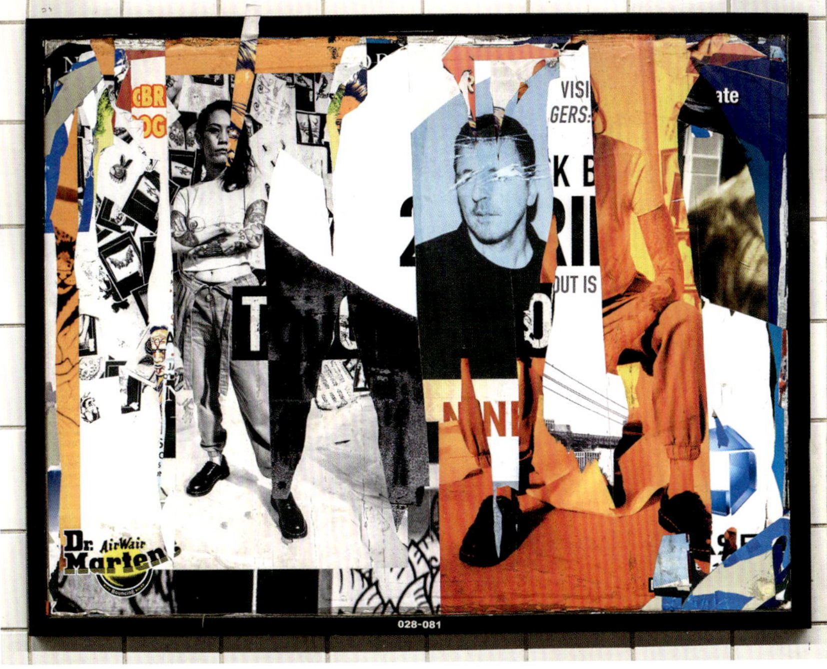

028-081

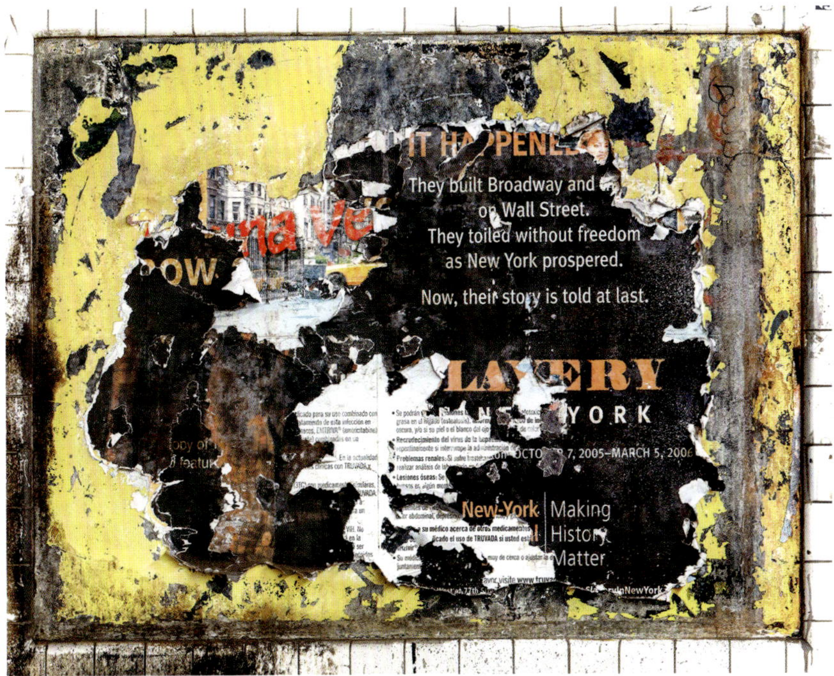

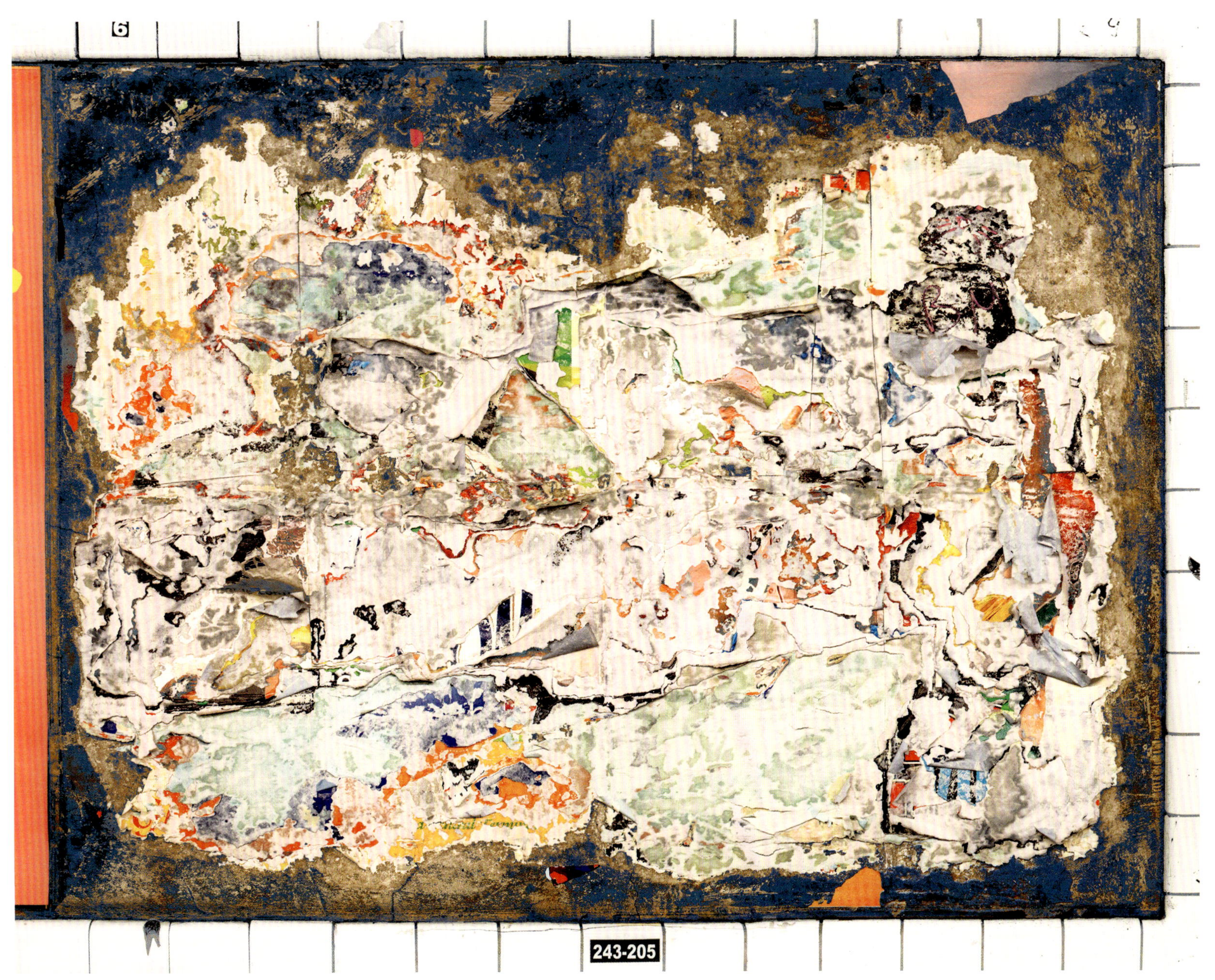

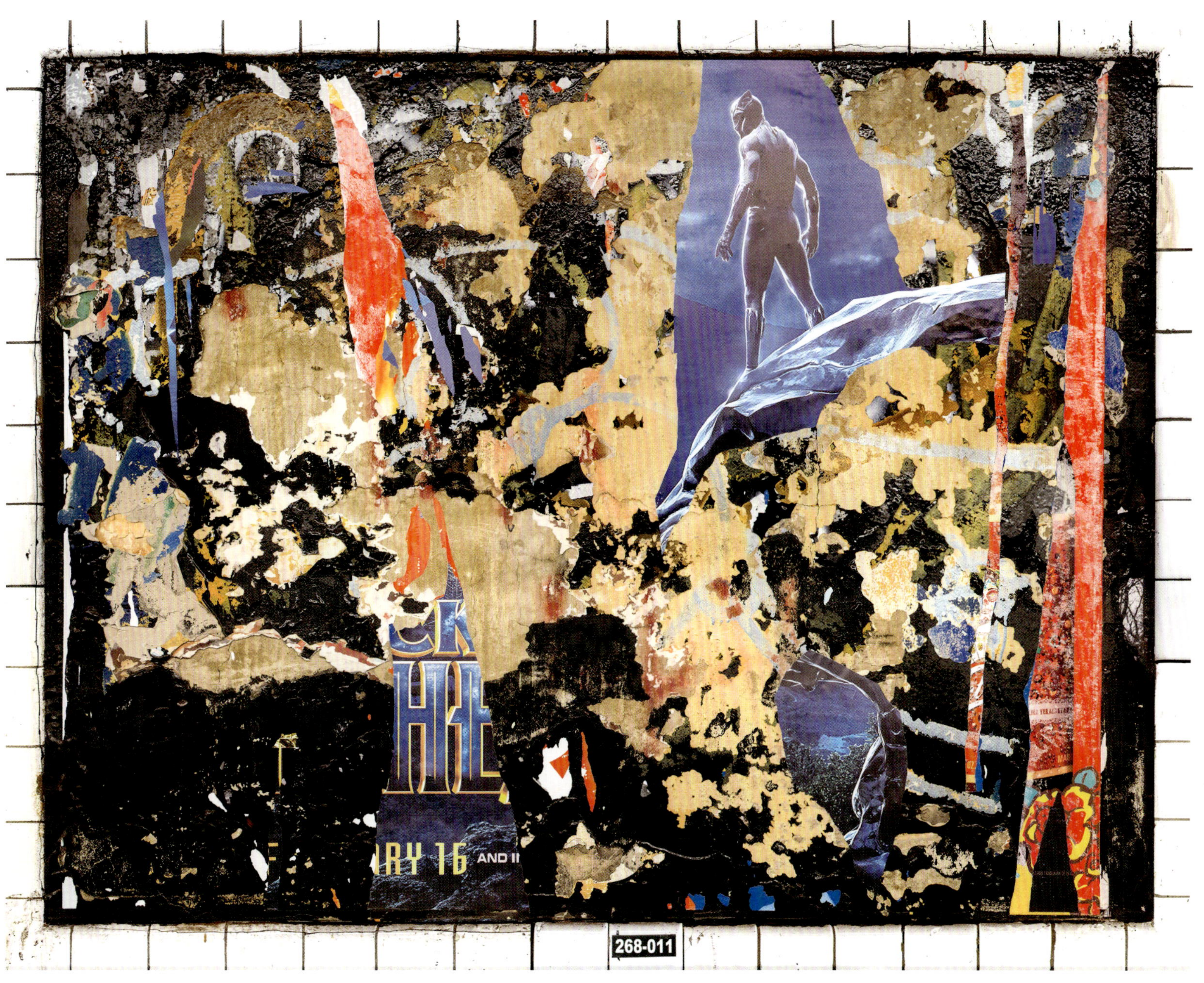
CK
H
RY 16 AND II

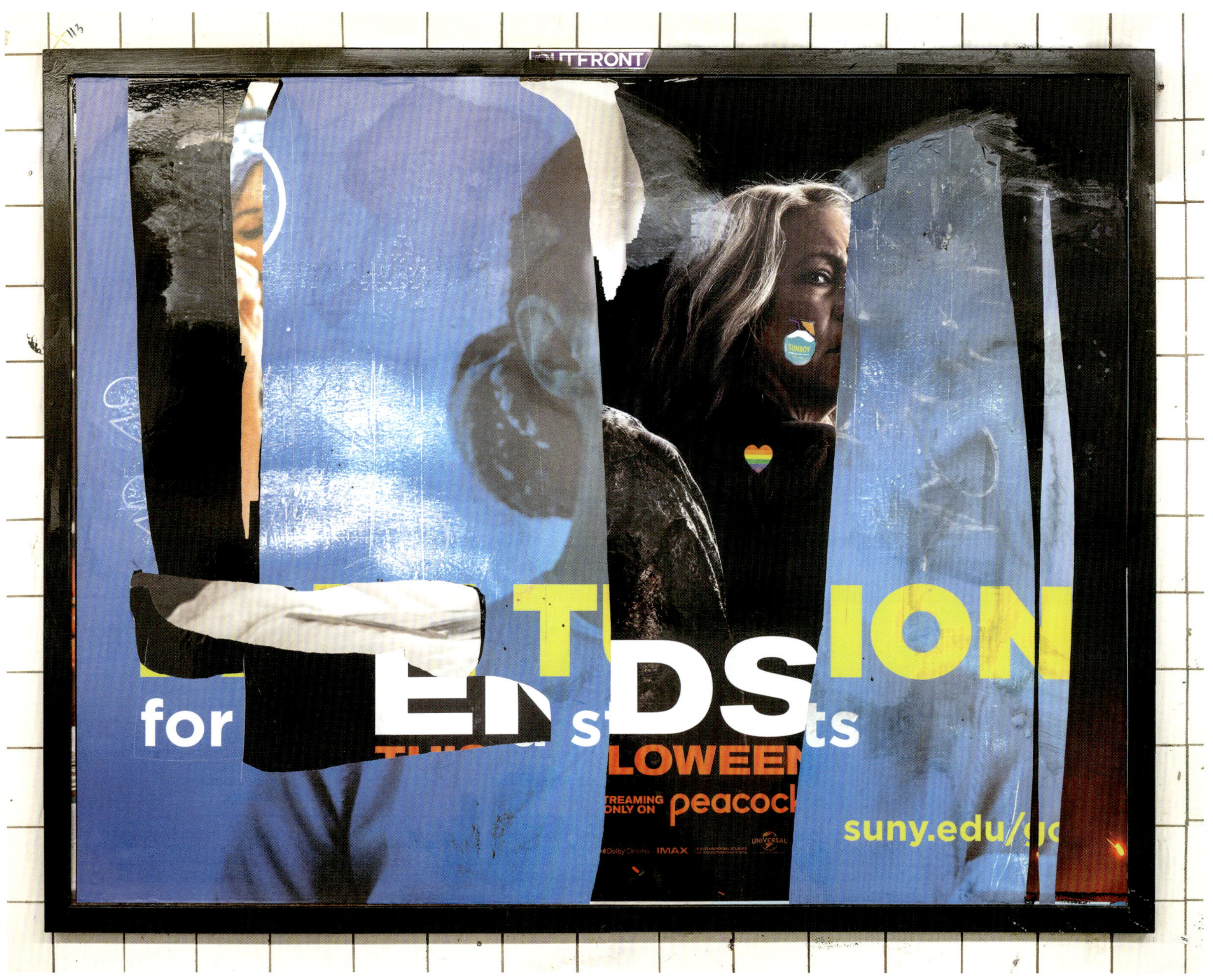
OUTFRONT
for
TUITION
ENDS
for students
HALLOWEEN
STREAMING
ONLY ON peacock
suny.edu/go
IMAX
UNIVERSAL

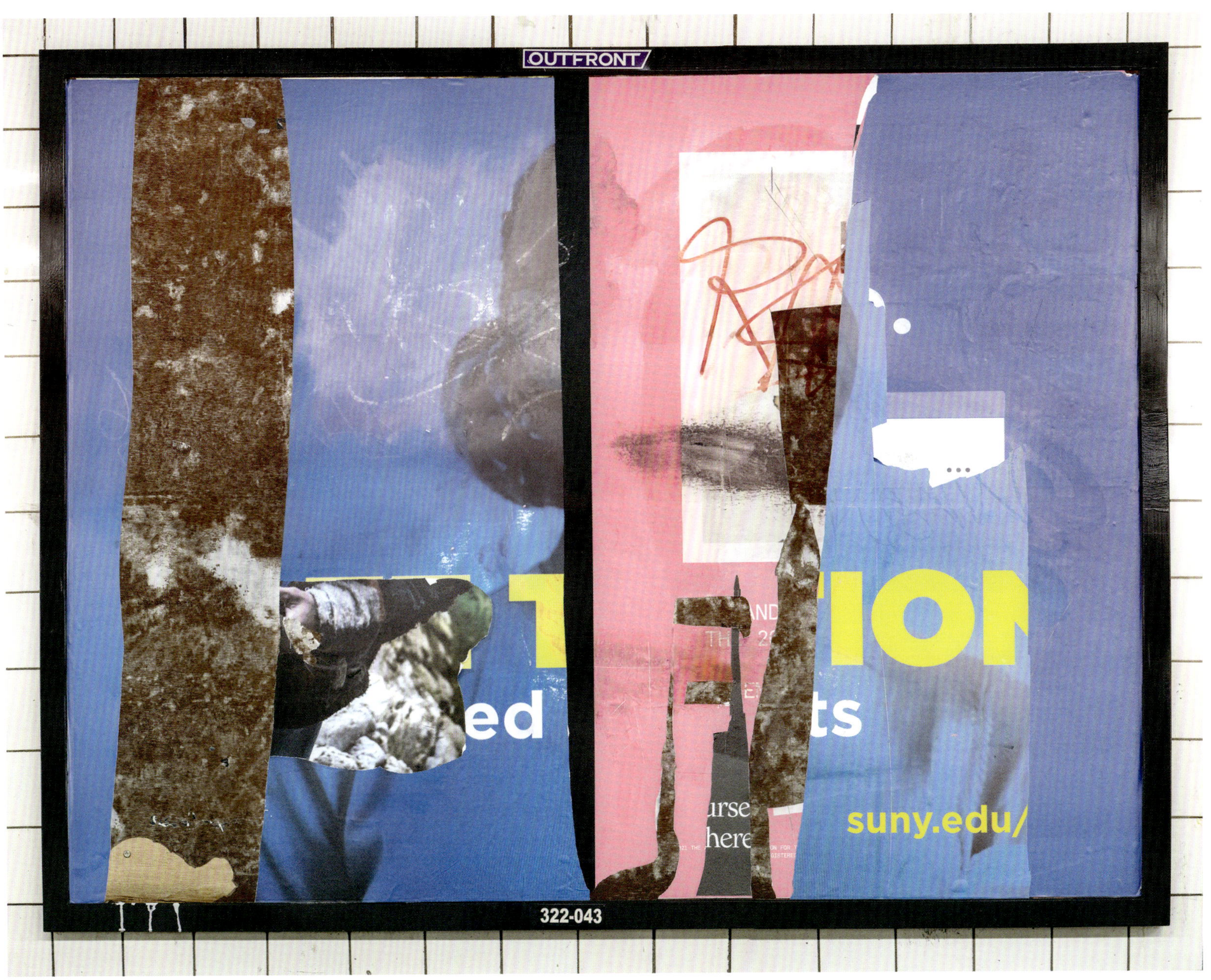
OUTFRONT
TION
ed
ts
AND
urse
here
suny.edu/
322-043

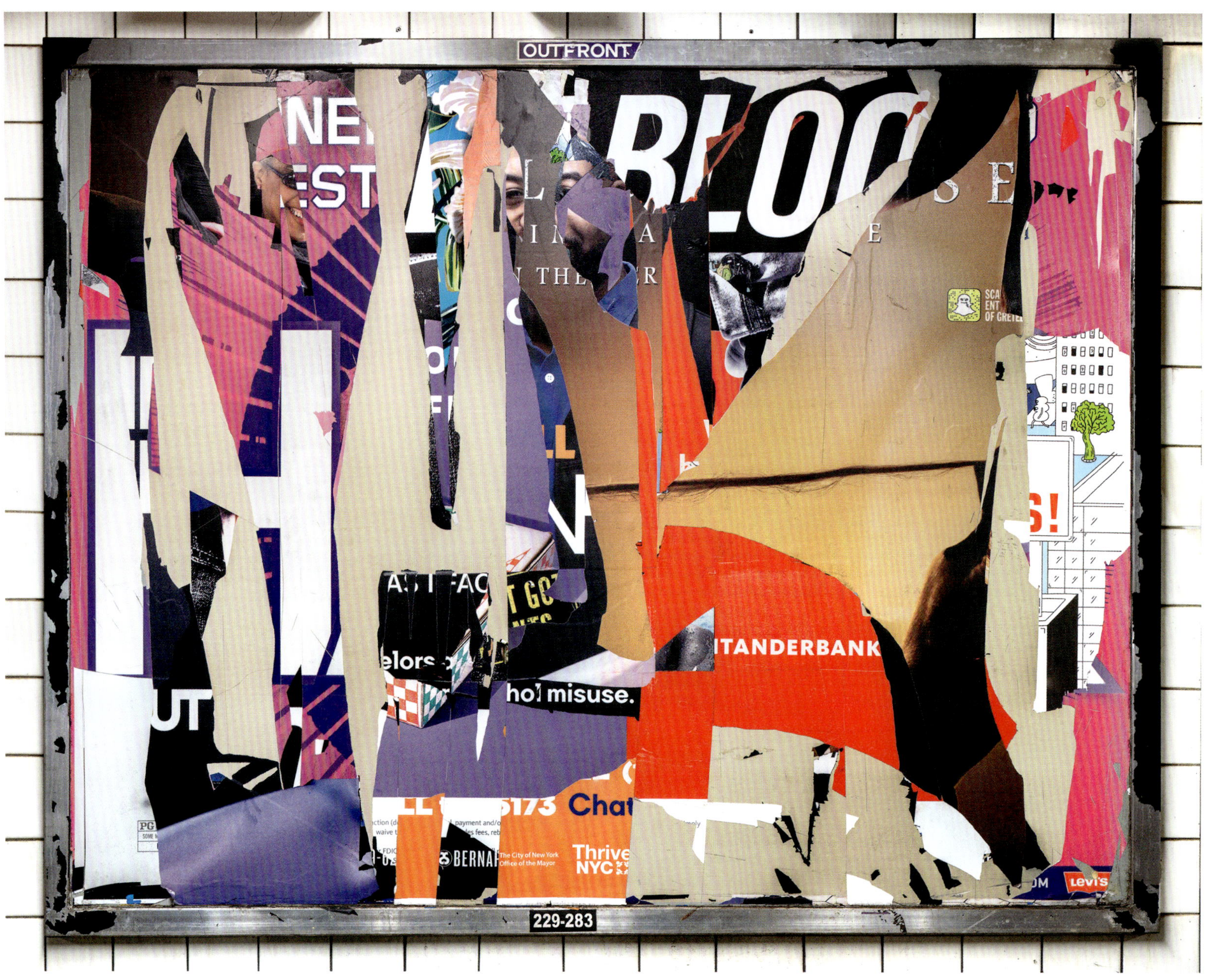

OUTFRONT
NE
EST
BLOO
E
THE
TANDERBANK
elors
hol misuse.
173 Chat
BERNA
The City of New York
Office of the Mayor
Thrive
NYC
Levi's
229-283

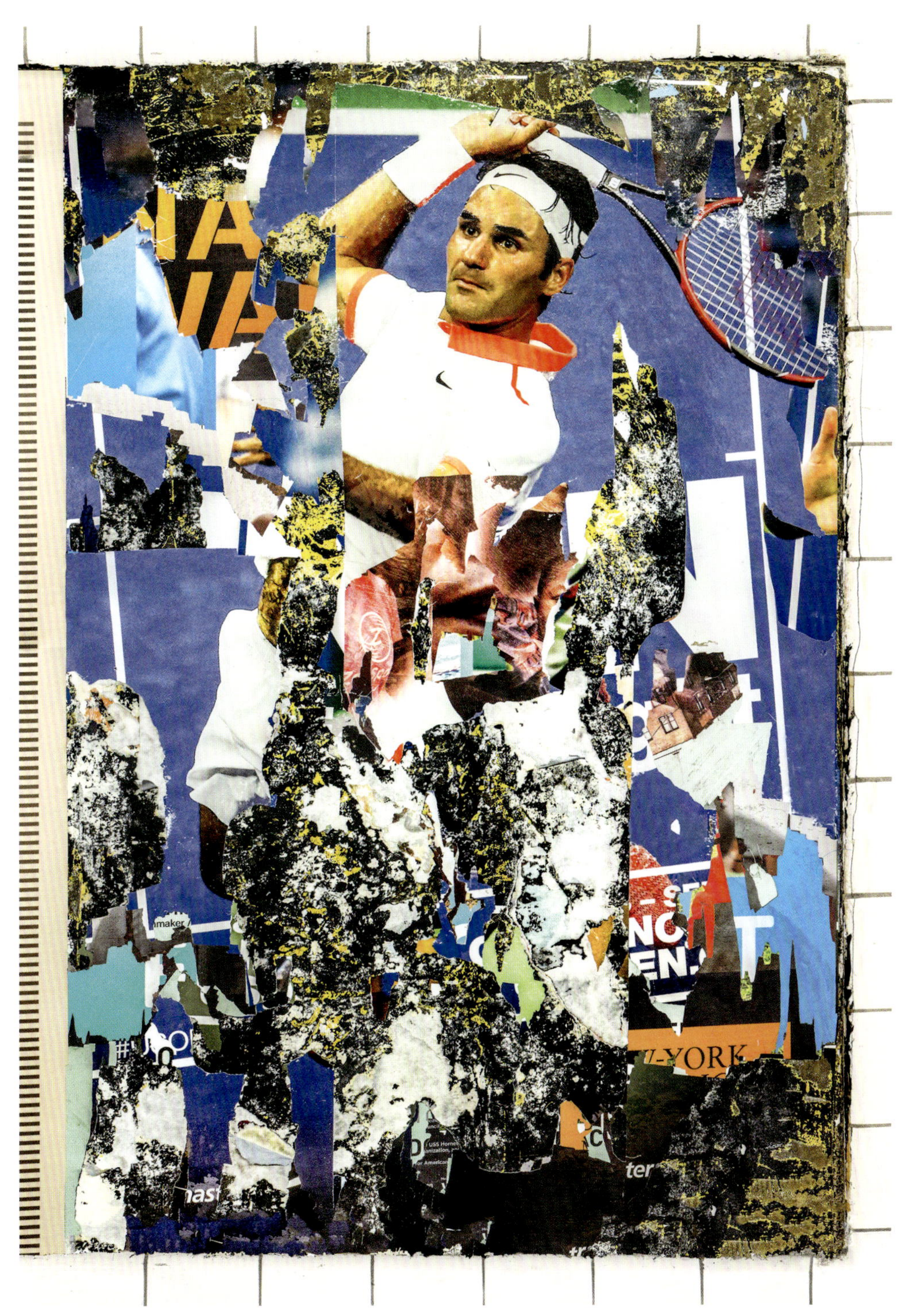

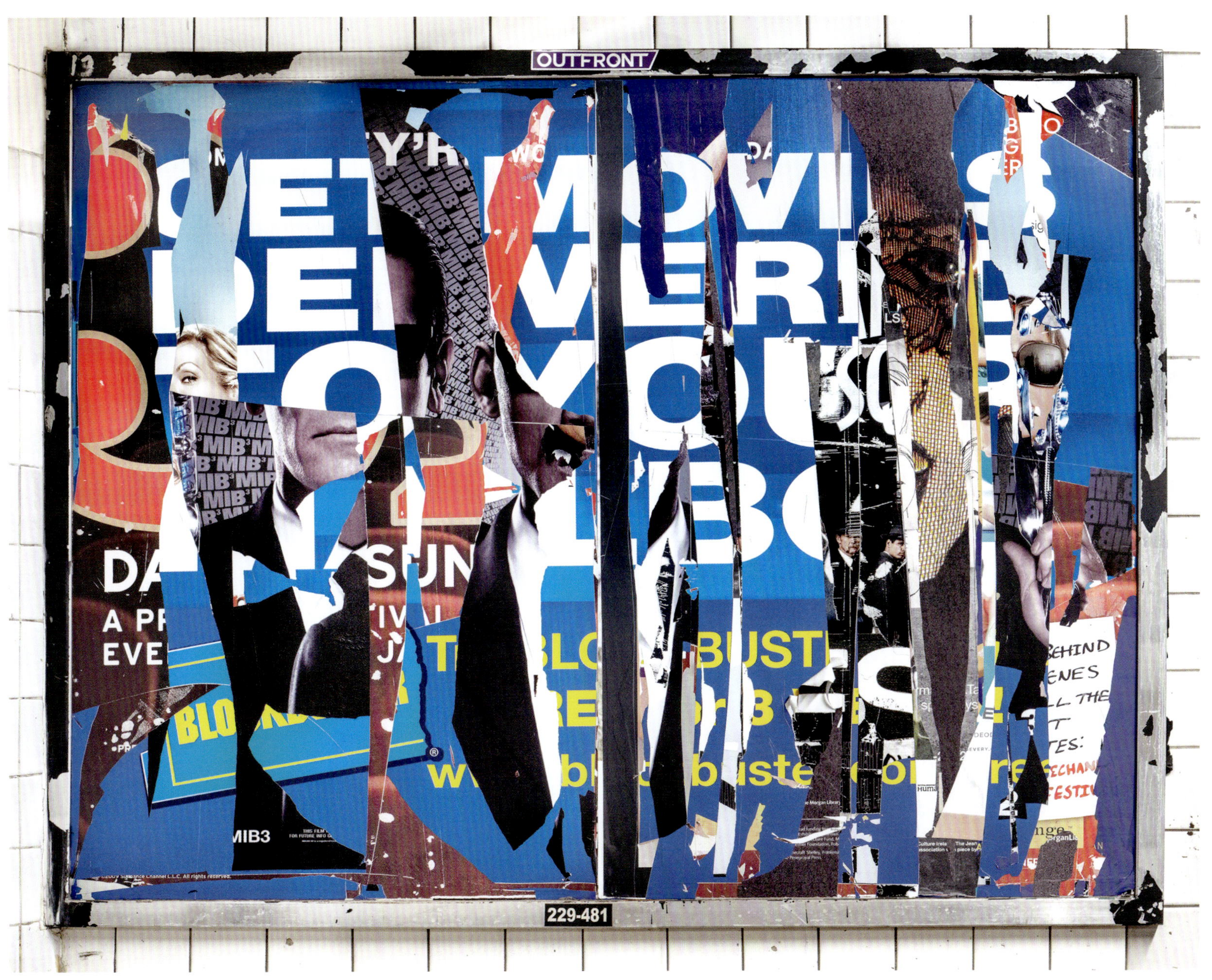
OUTFRONT
GET MOVIES
DELIVERED
TO YOUR
MAILBOX
DA SUN
A PR
EVE
BLO
MIB3
BLOCKBUSTER
229-481

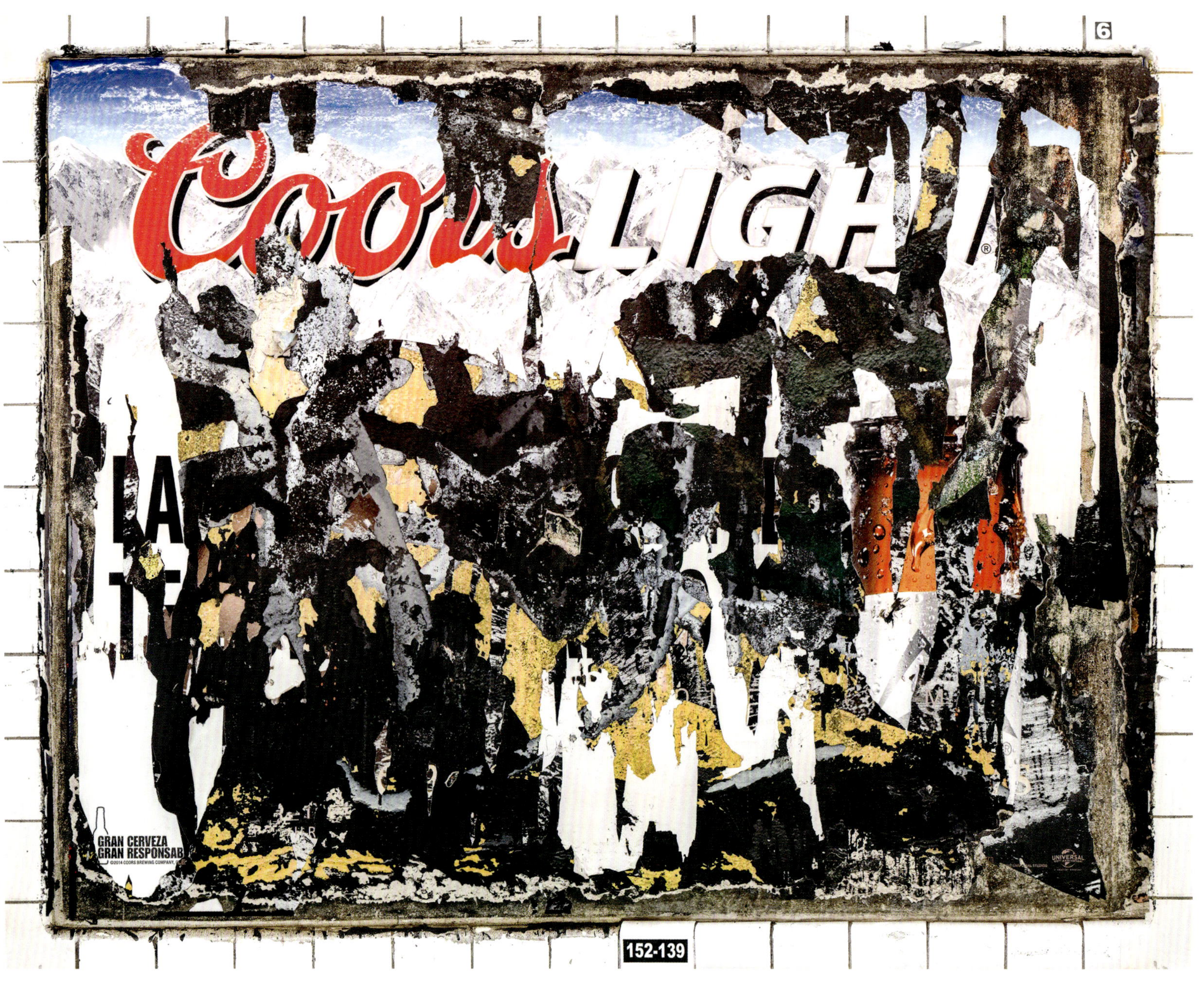
6
COORS LIGHT
LA
GRAN CERVEZA
GRAN RESPONSAB
©2014 COORS BREWING COMPANY,
UNIVERSAL
152-139

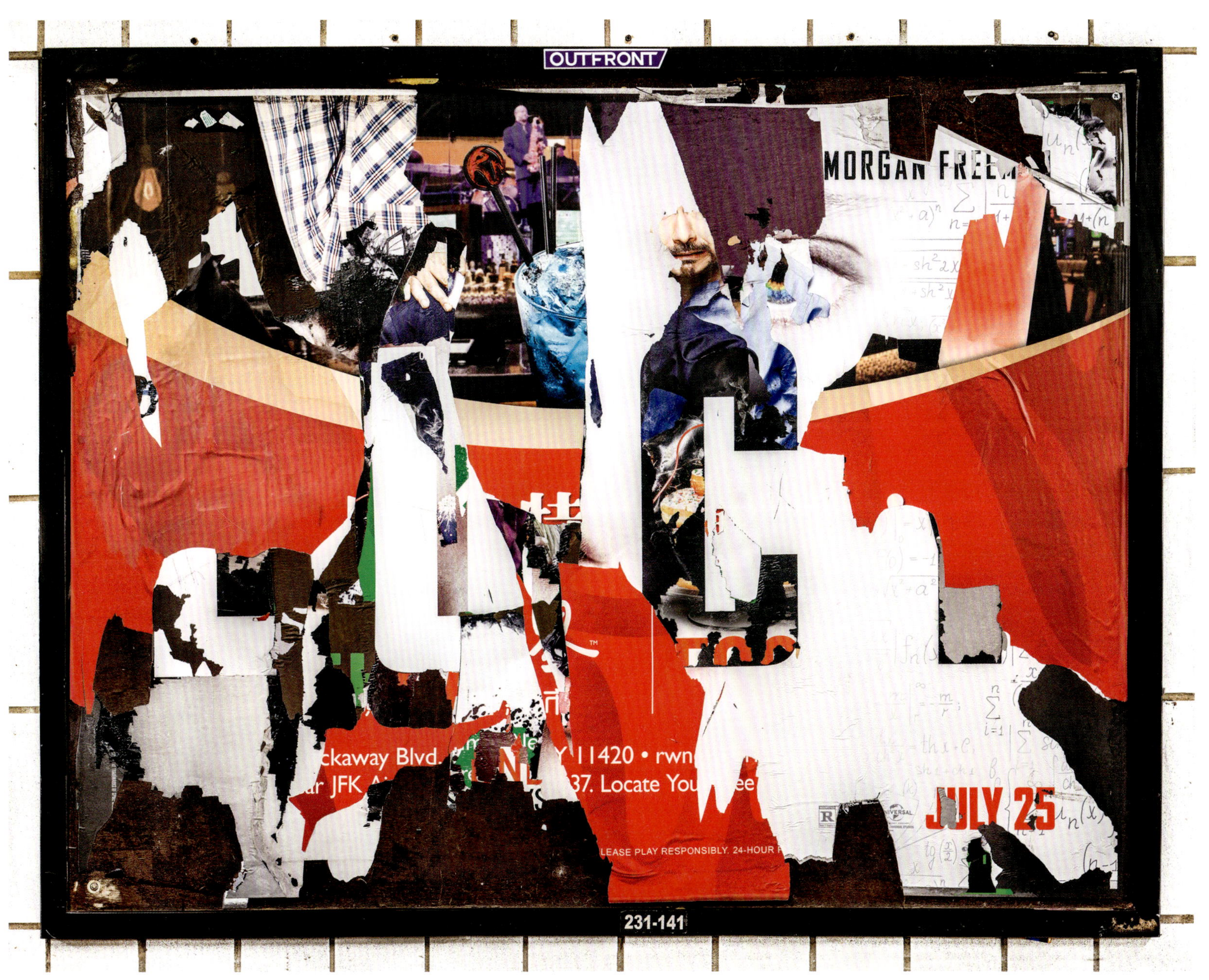
OUTFRONT
MORGAN FREEM
ckaway Blvd.
ar JFK A
Y 11420 • rwn
37. Locate You
JULY 25
LEASE PLAY RESPONSIBLY. 24-HOUR
231-141

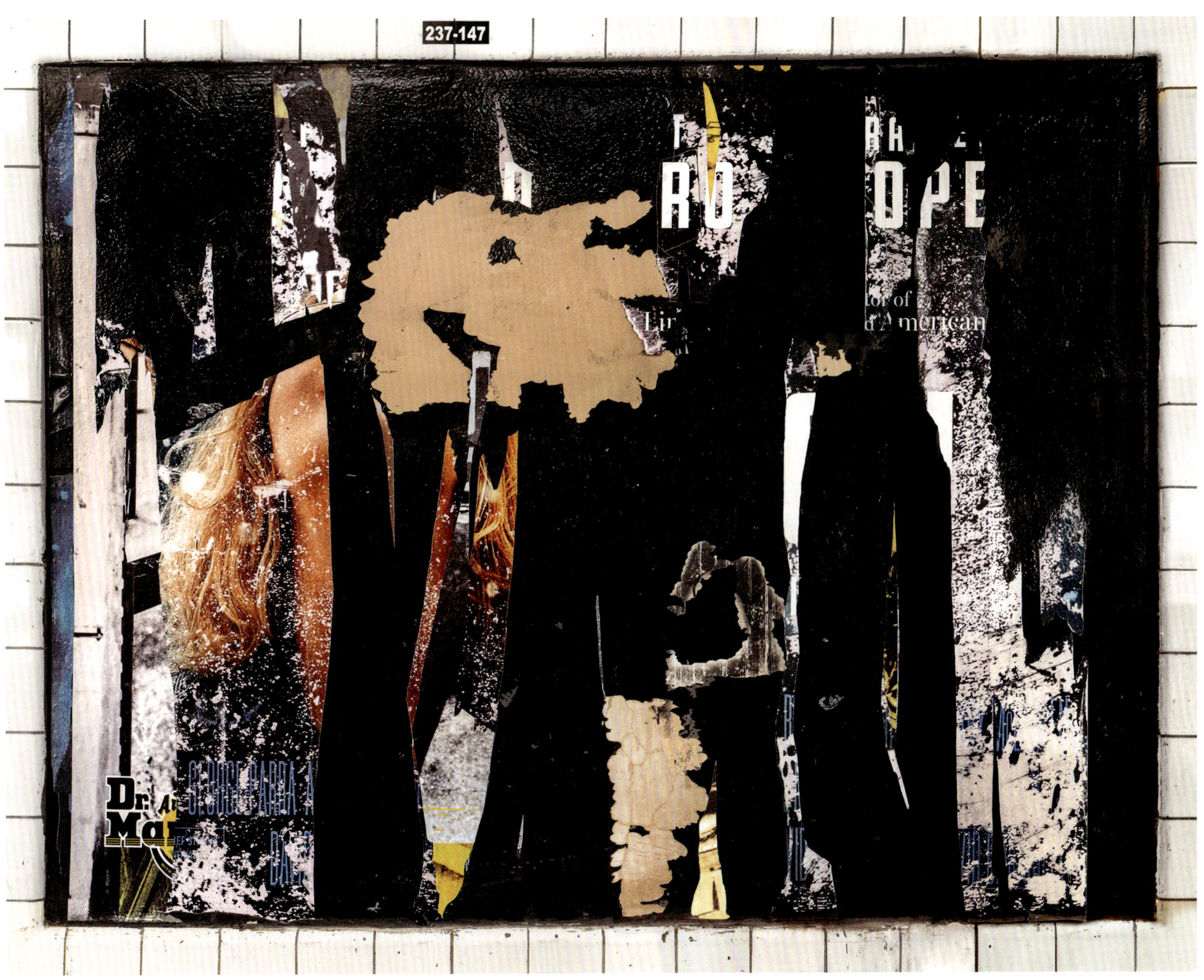
237-147
RO
DPE
of
d'American
Dr.
Ma

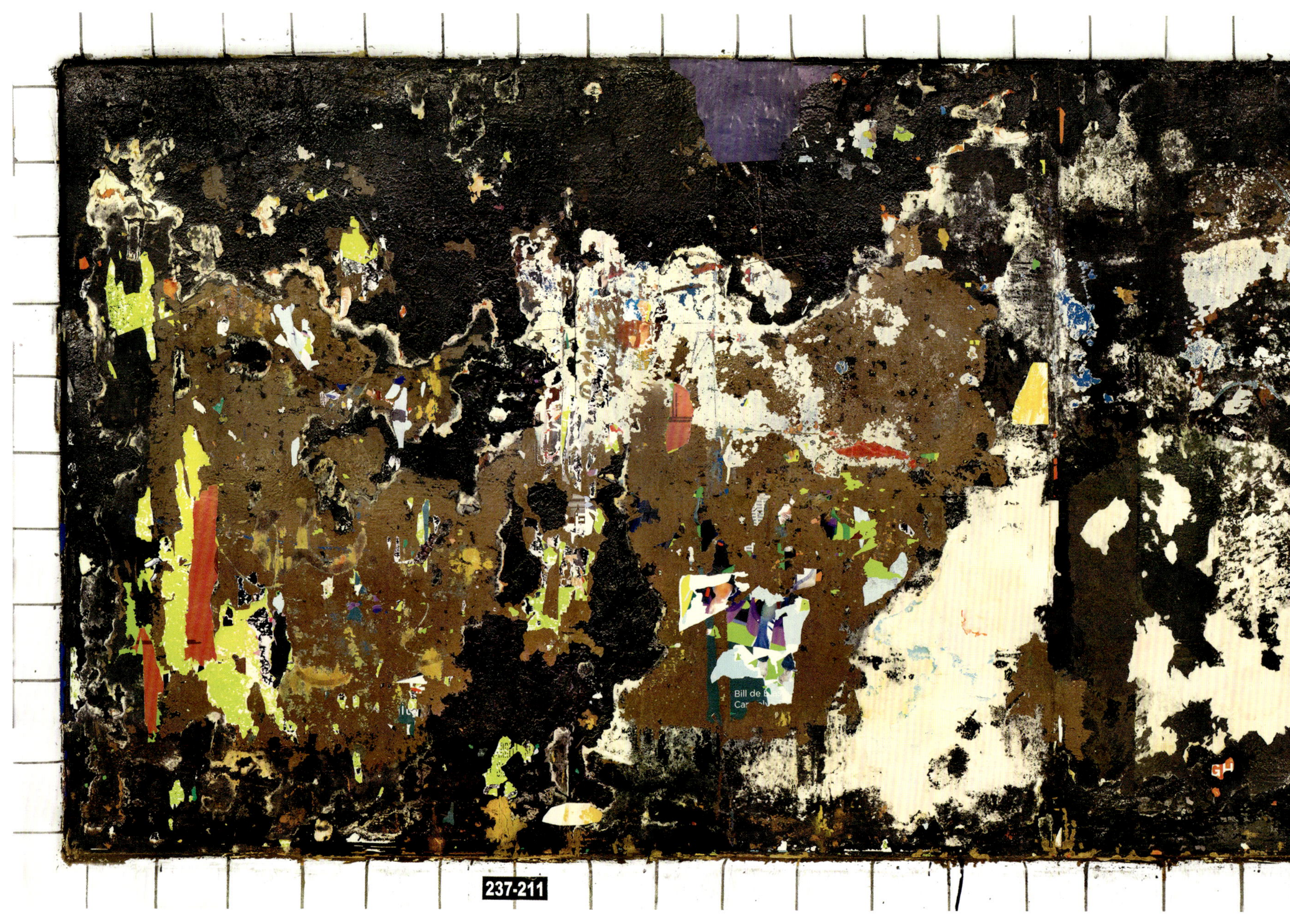
237-211

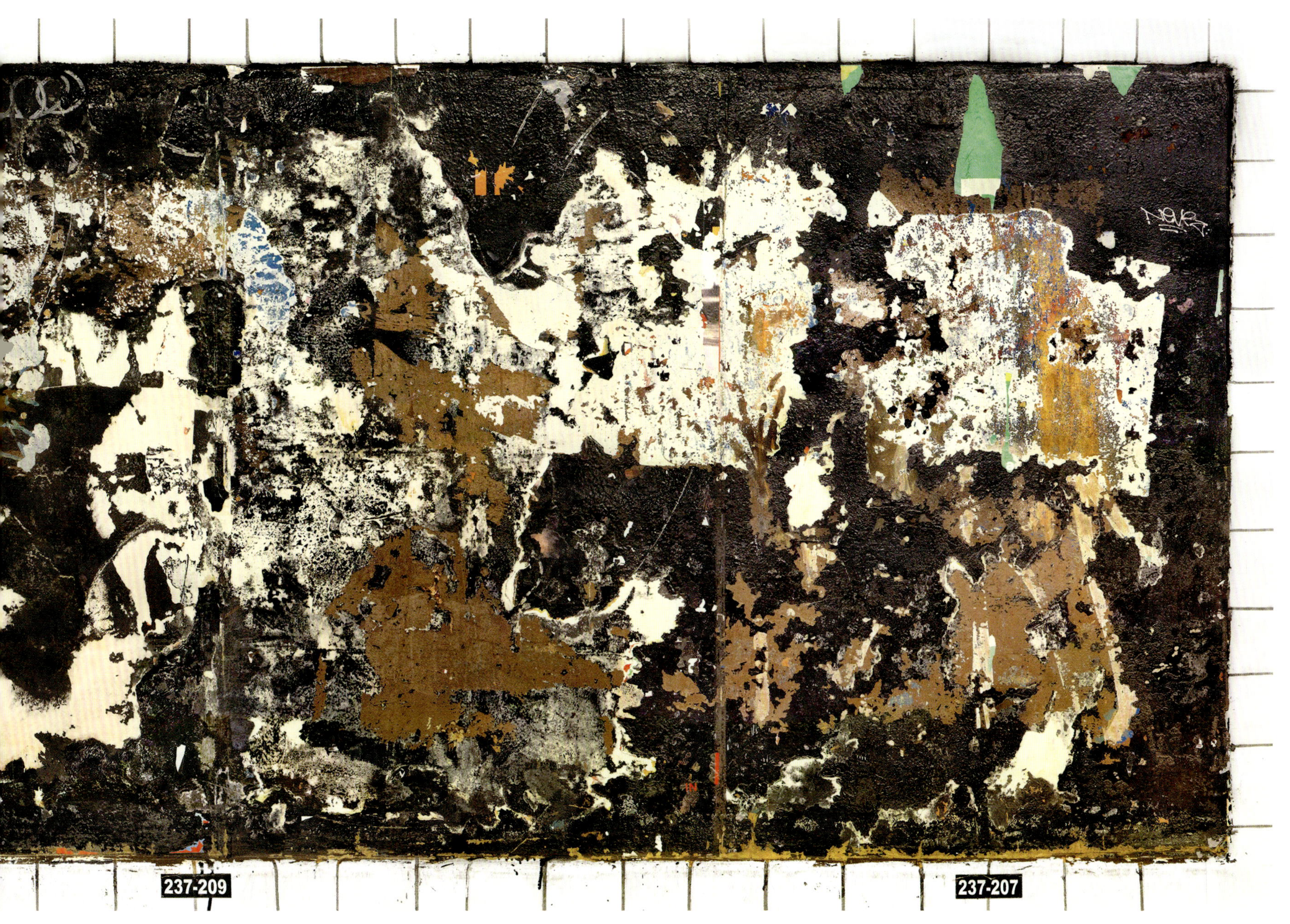

237-209
237-207

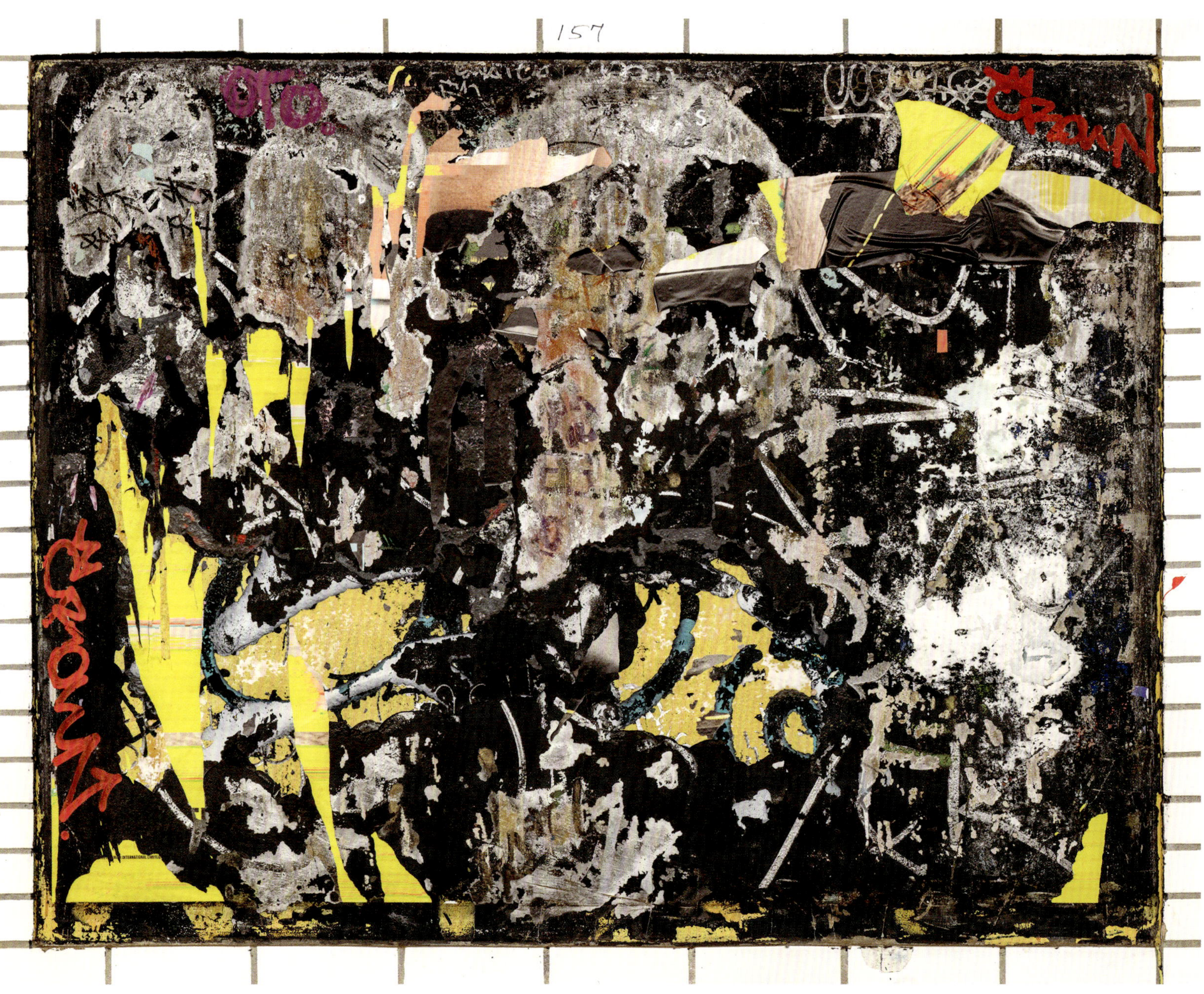

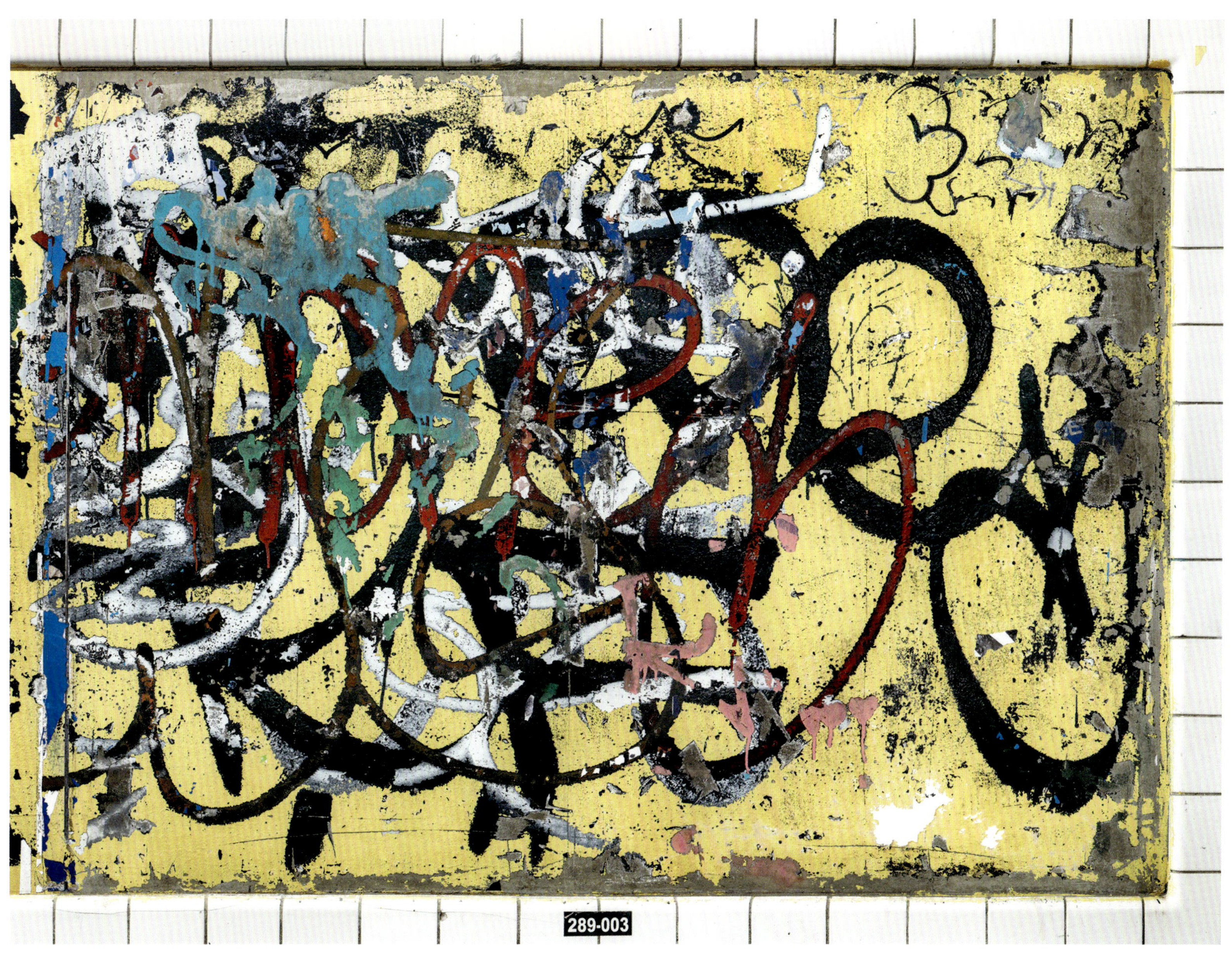
289-003

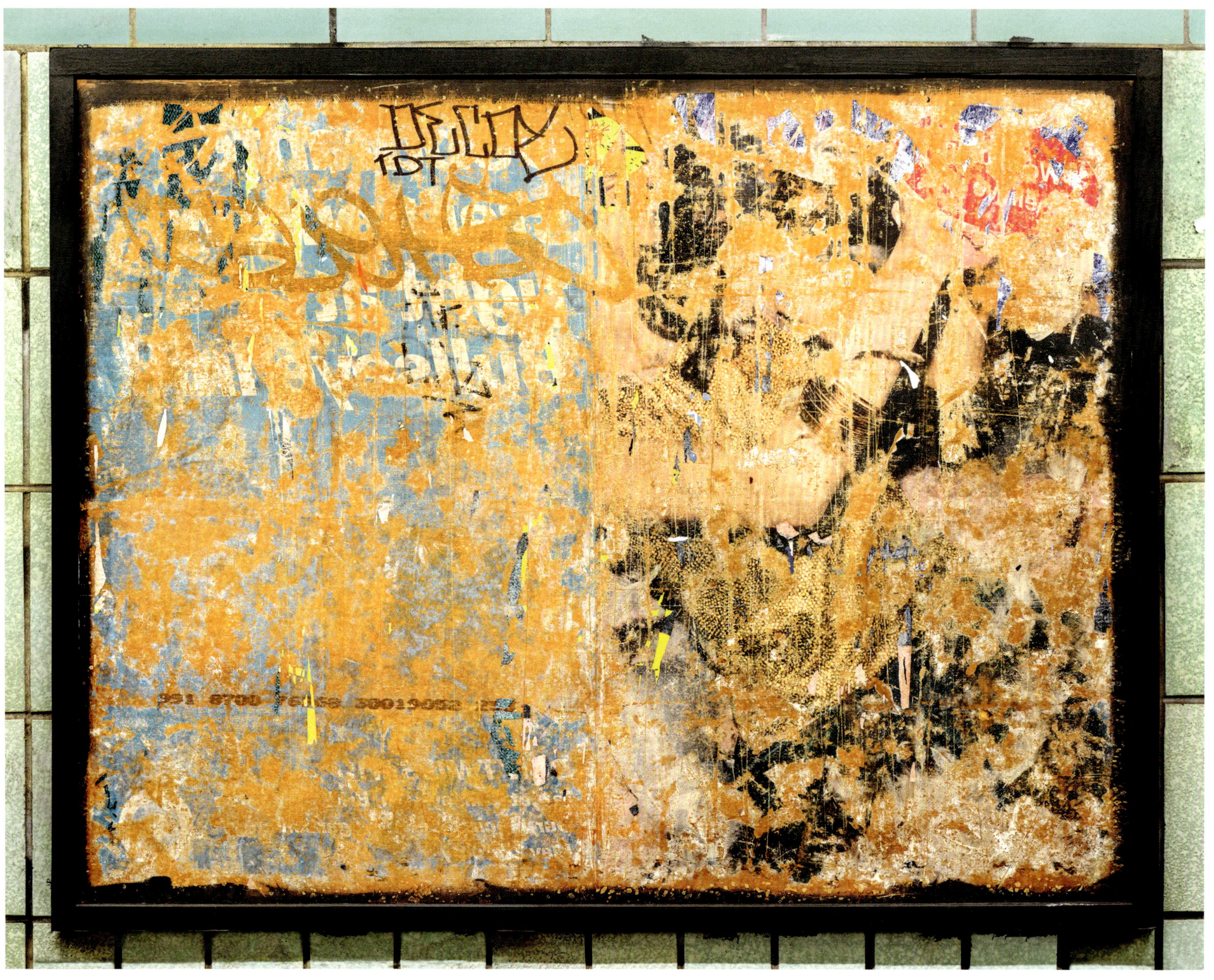

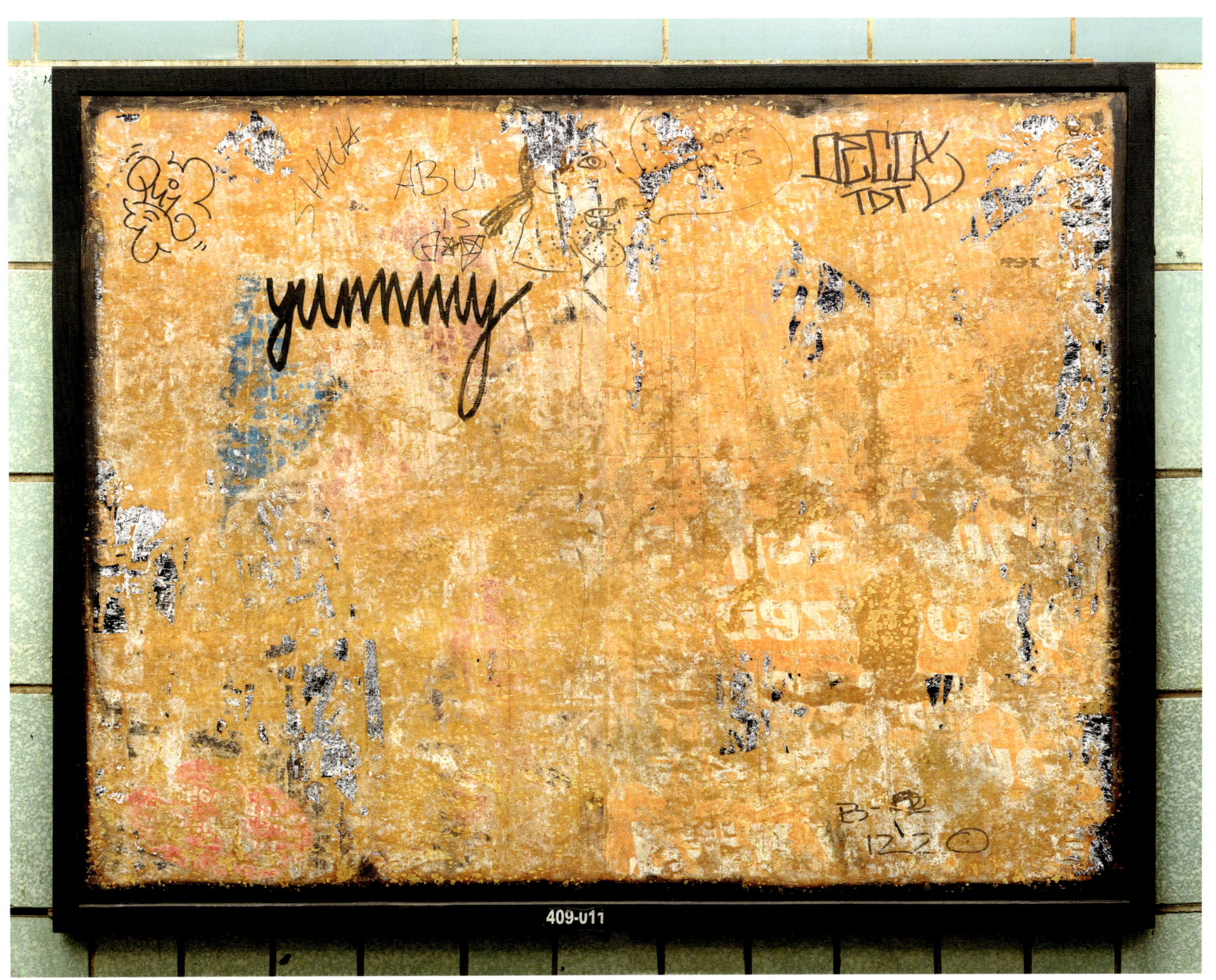

ABU
IS
yummy
DELTA
TDT
409-011

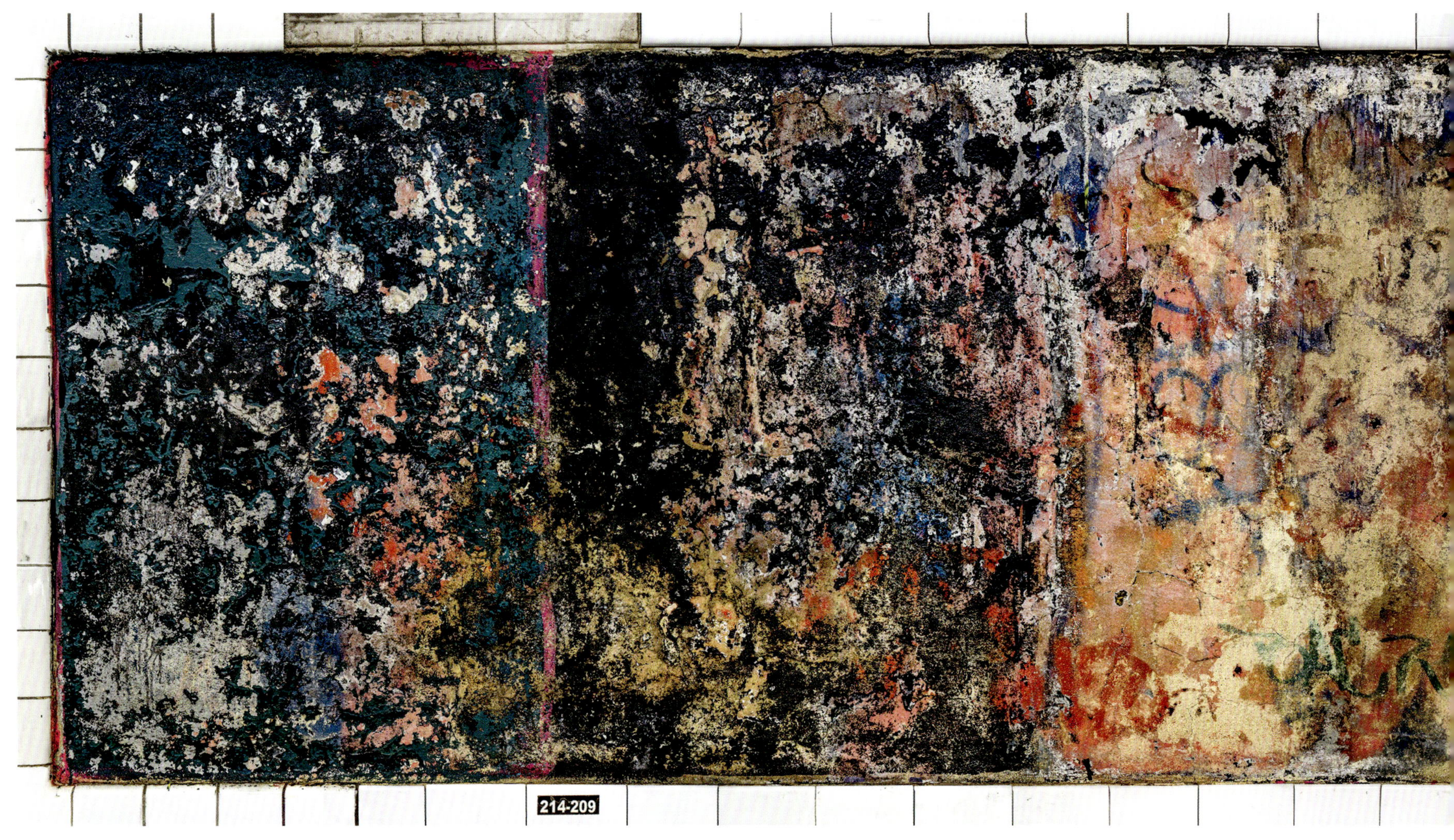

214-209

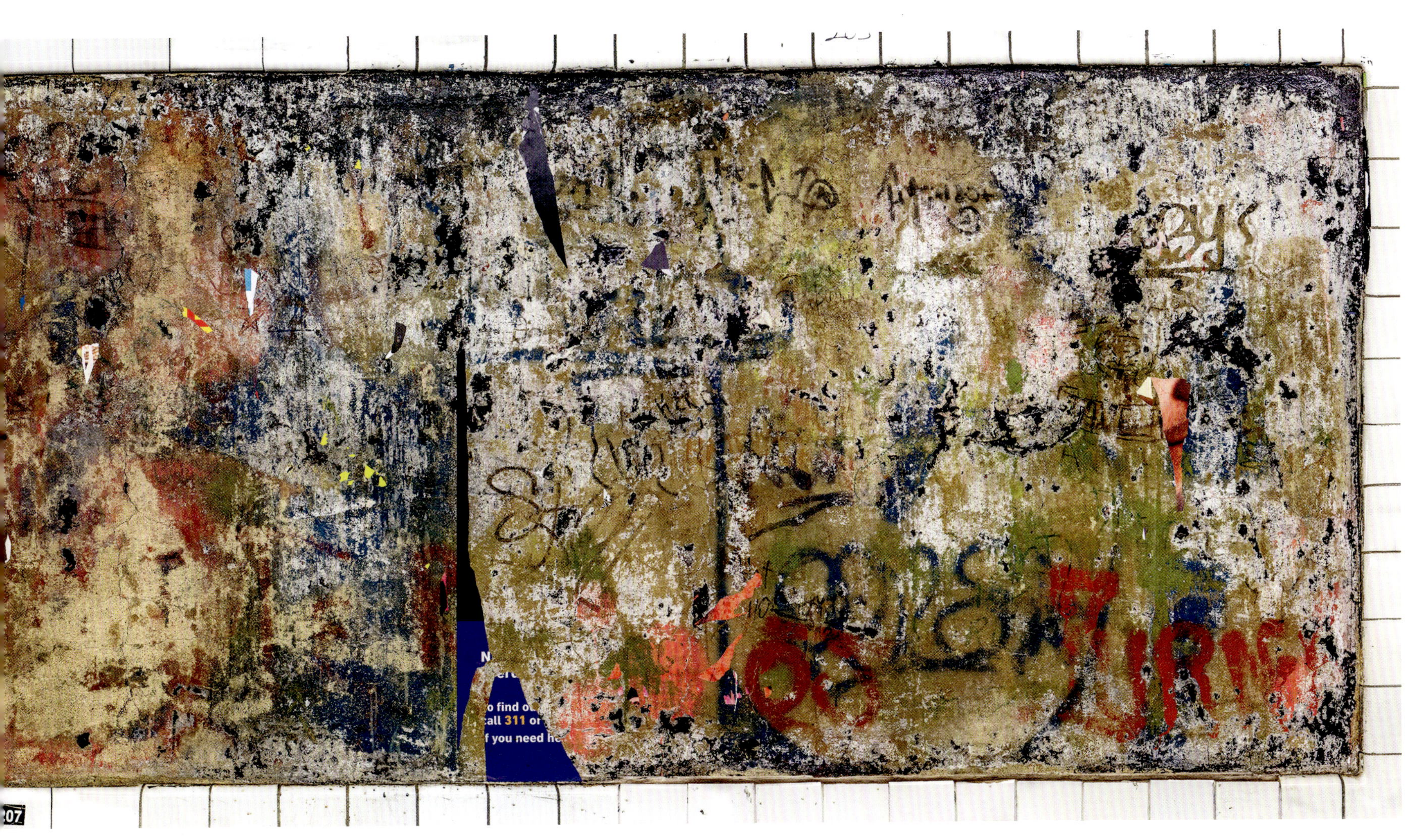

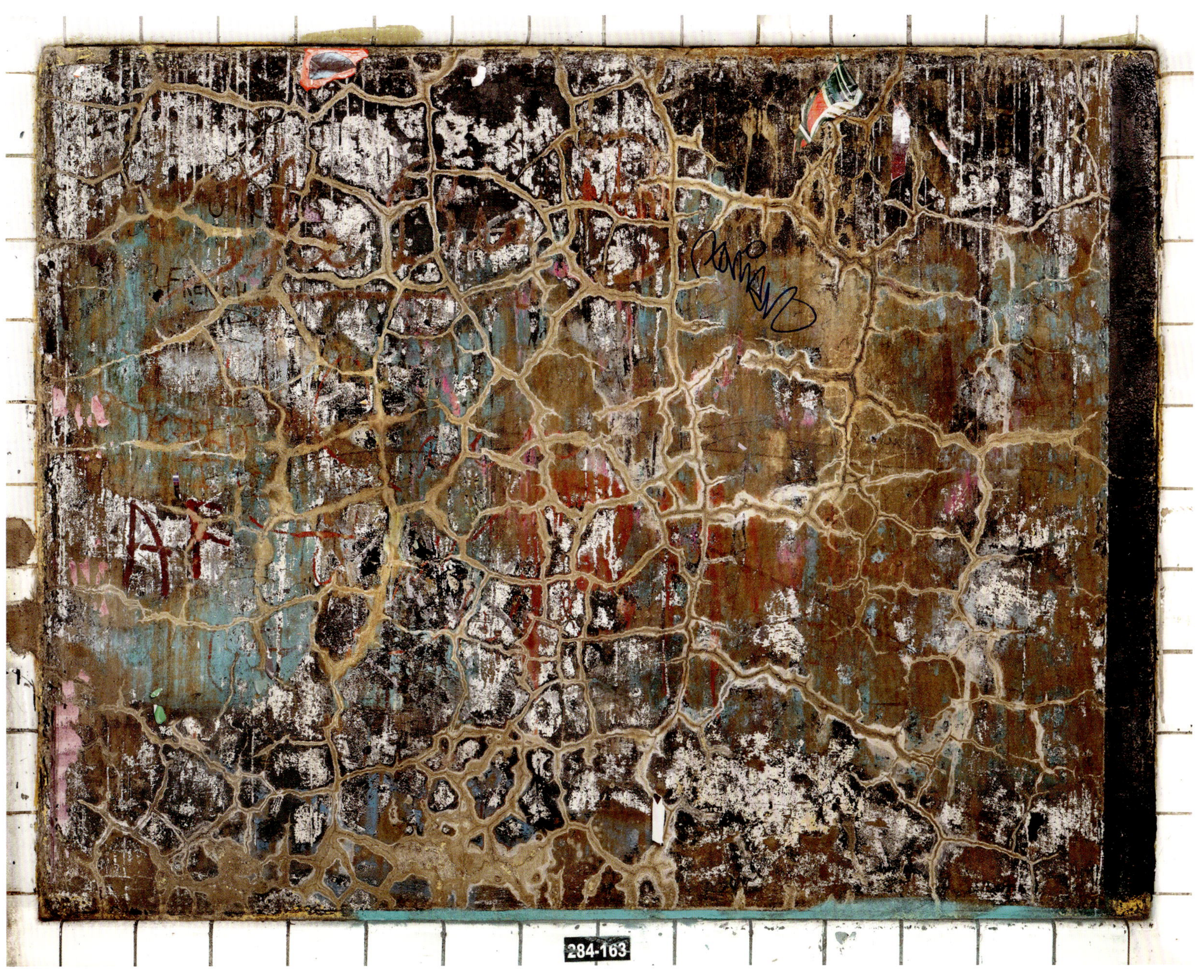
284-163

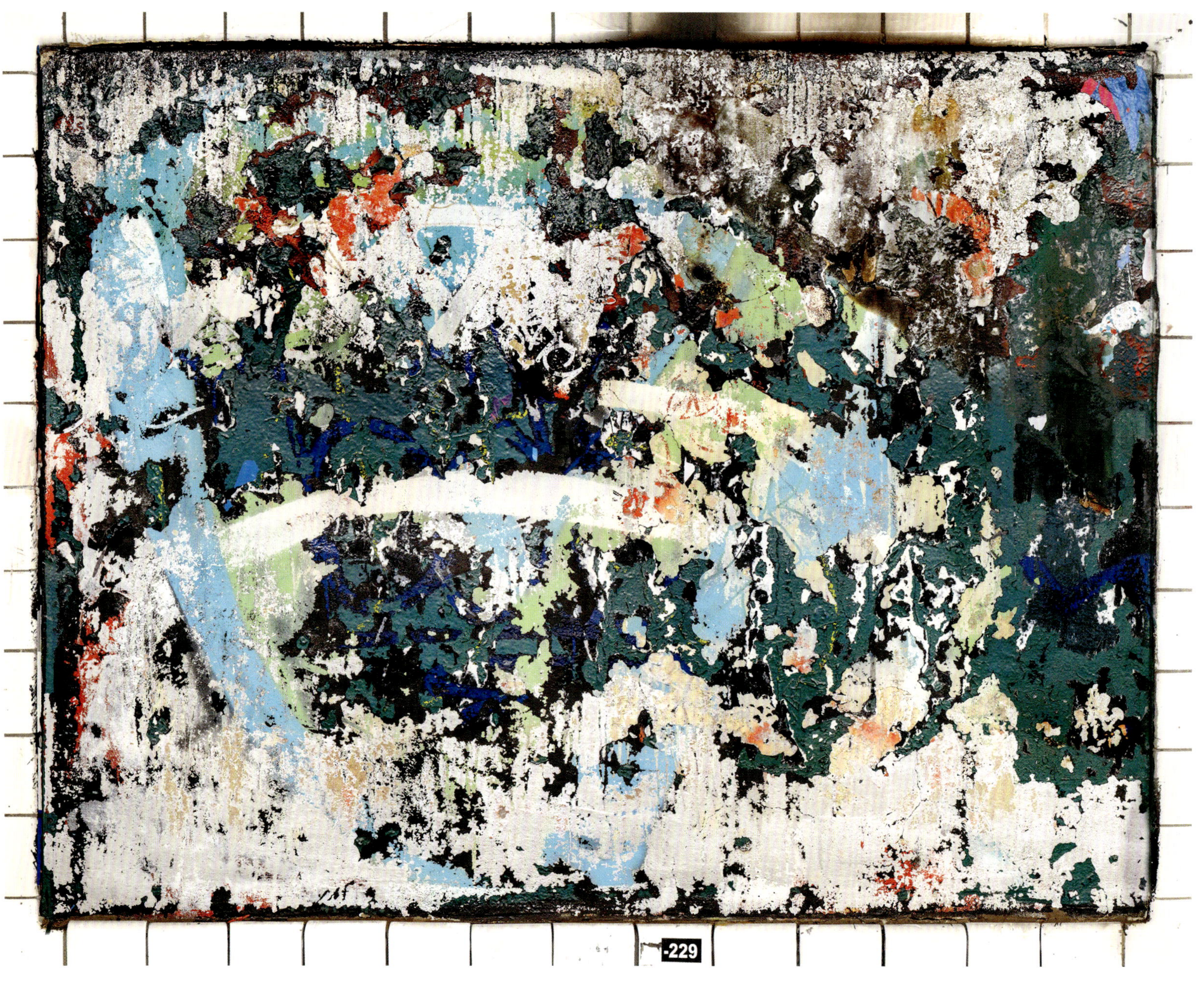

-229

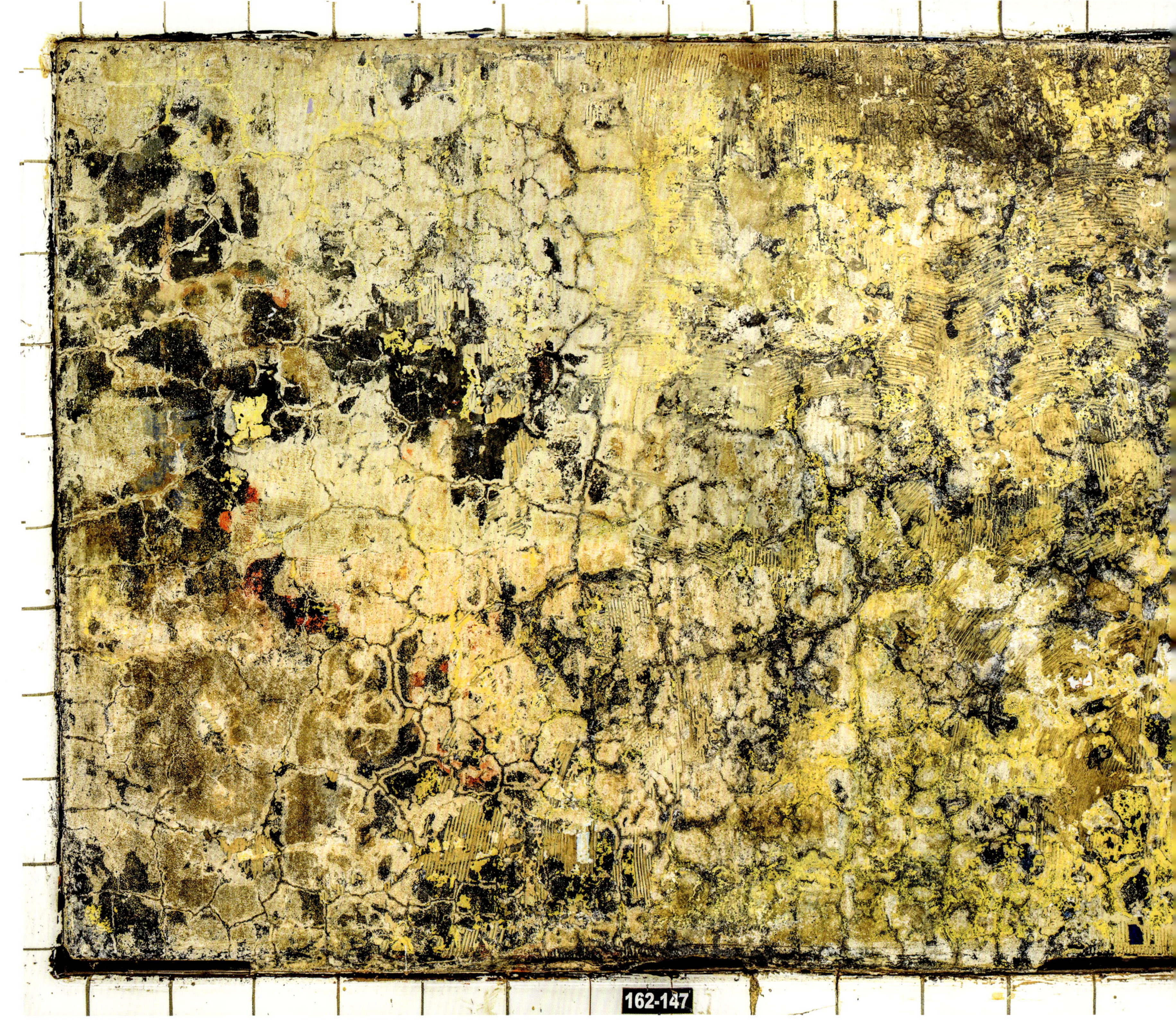

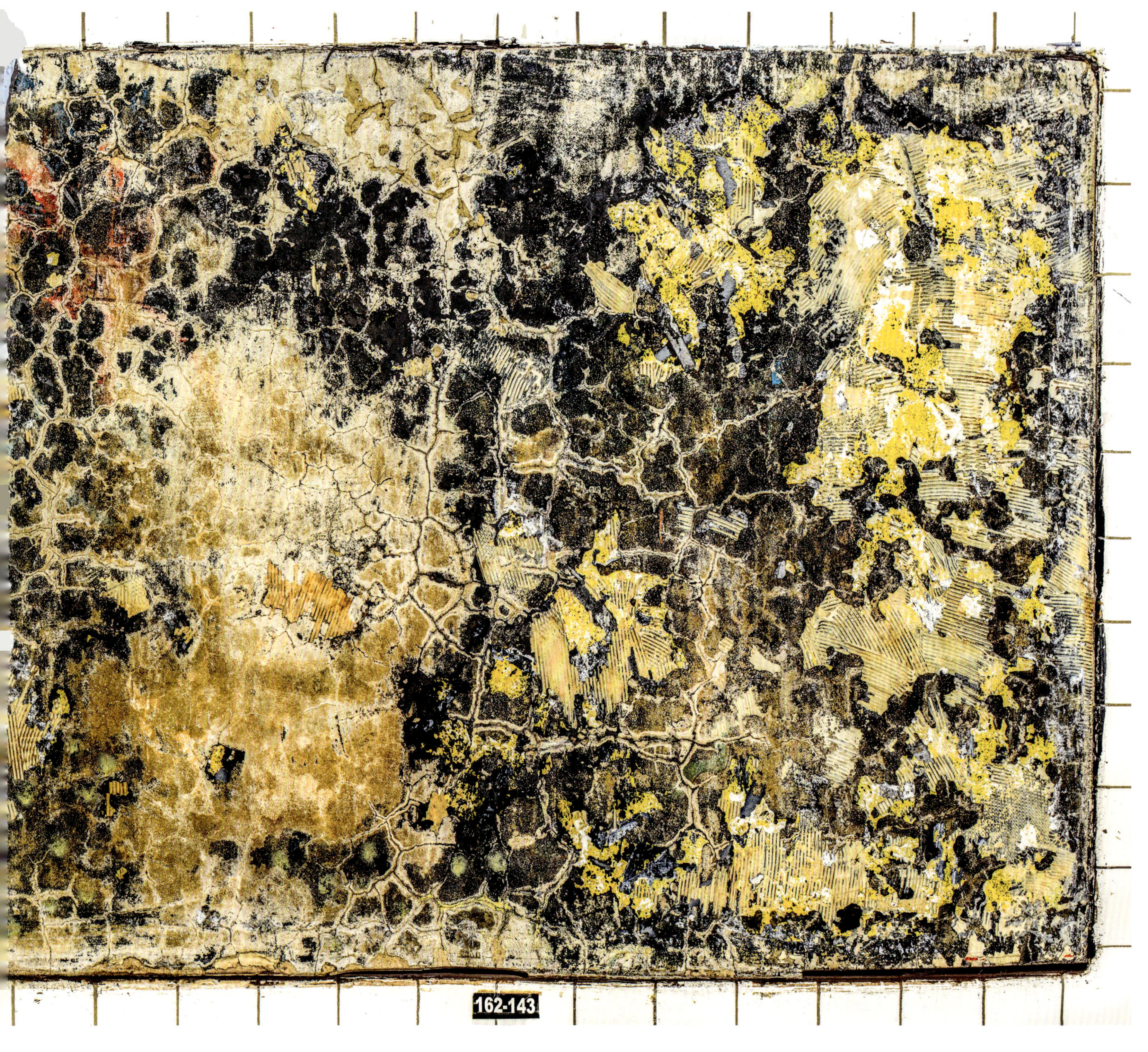

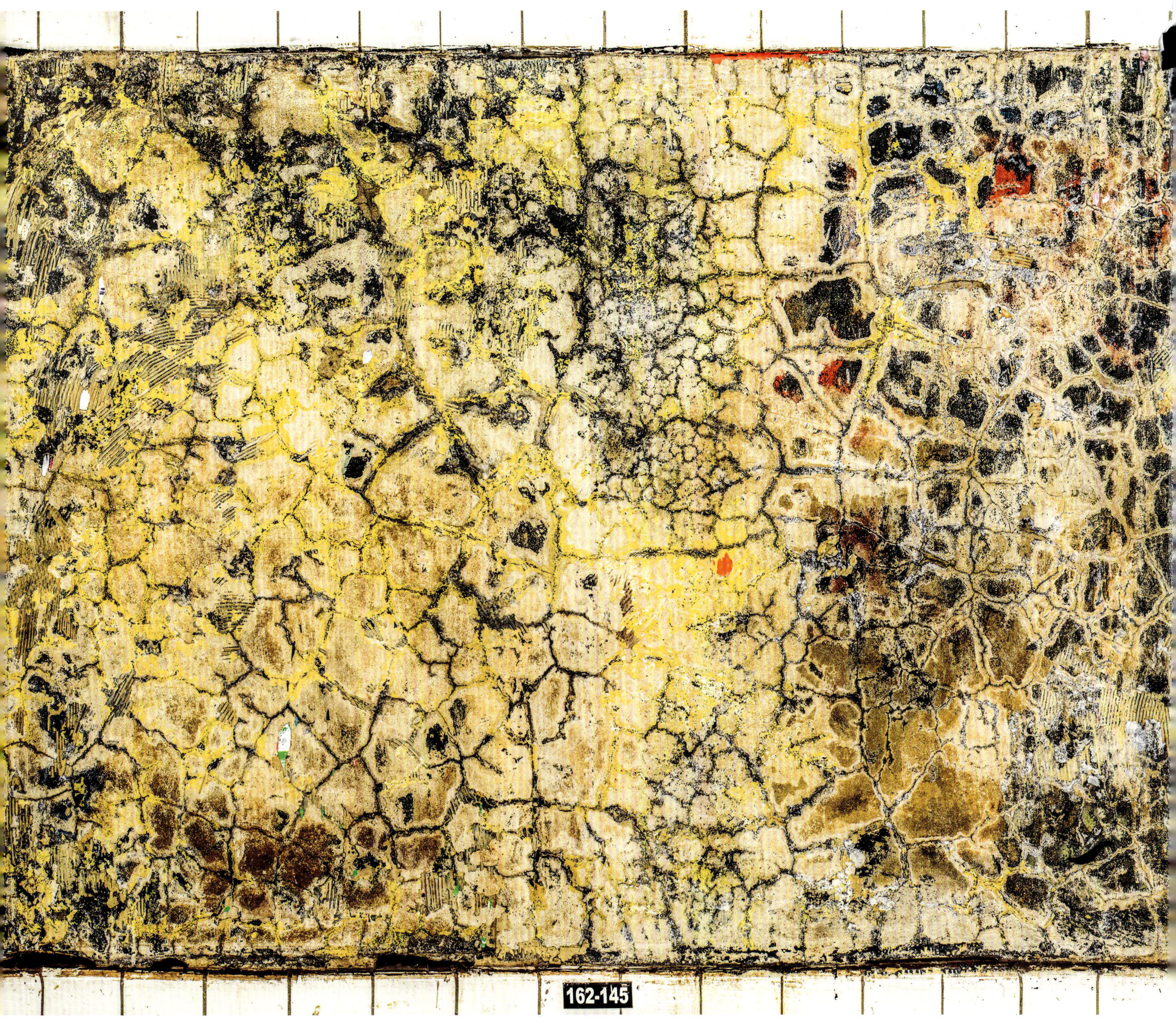
162-145

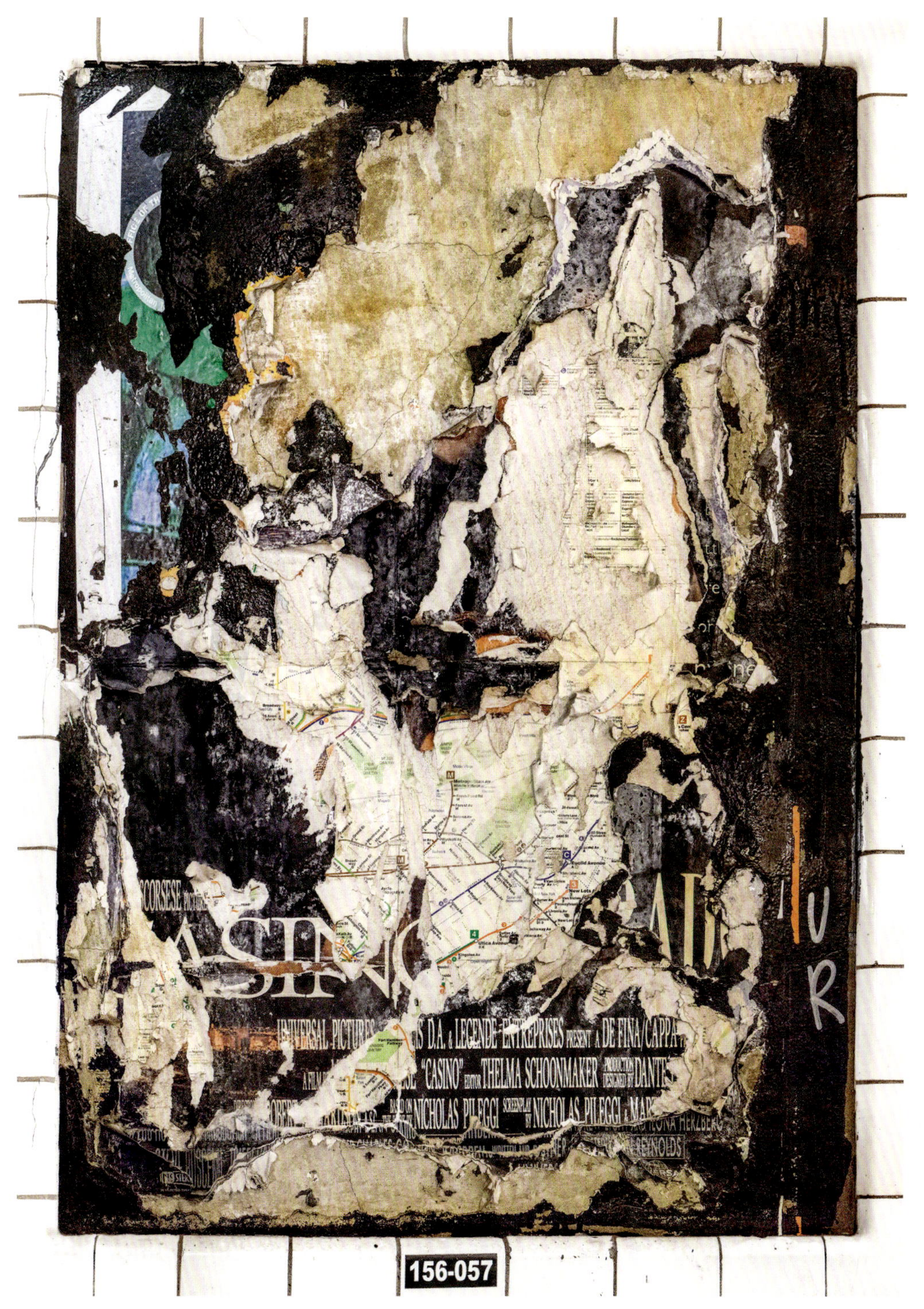
CORSESE PICTURES
ASINO
UNIVERSAL PICTURES ... IS D.A. & LEGENDE ENTREPRISES PRÉSENT A DE FINA/CAPPA
A FILM ... DE "CASINO" EDITOR THELMA SCHOONMAKER PRODUCTION DESIGNER DANTE
... NICHOLAS PILEGGI SCREENPLAY BY NICHOLAS PILEGGI & MAR...
REYNOLDS
156-057

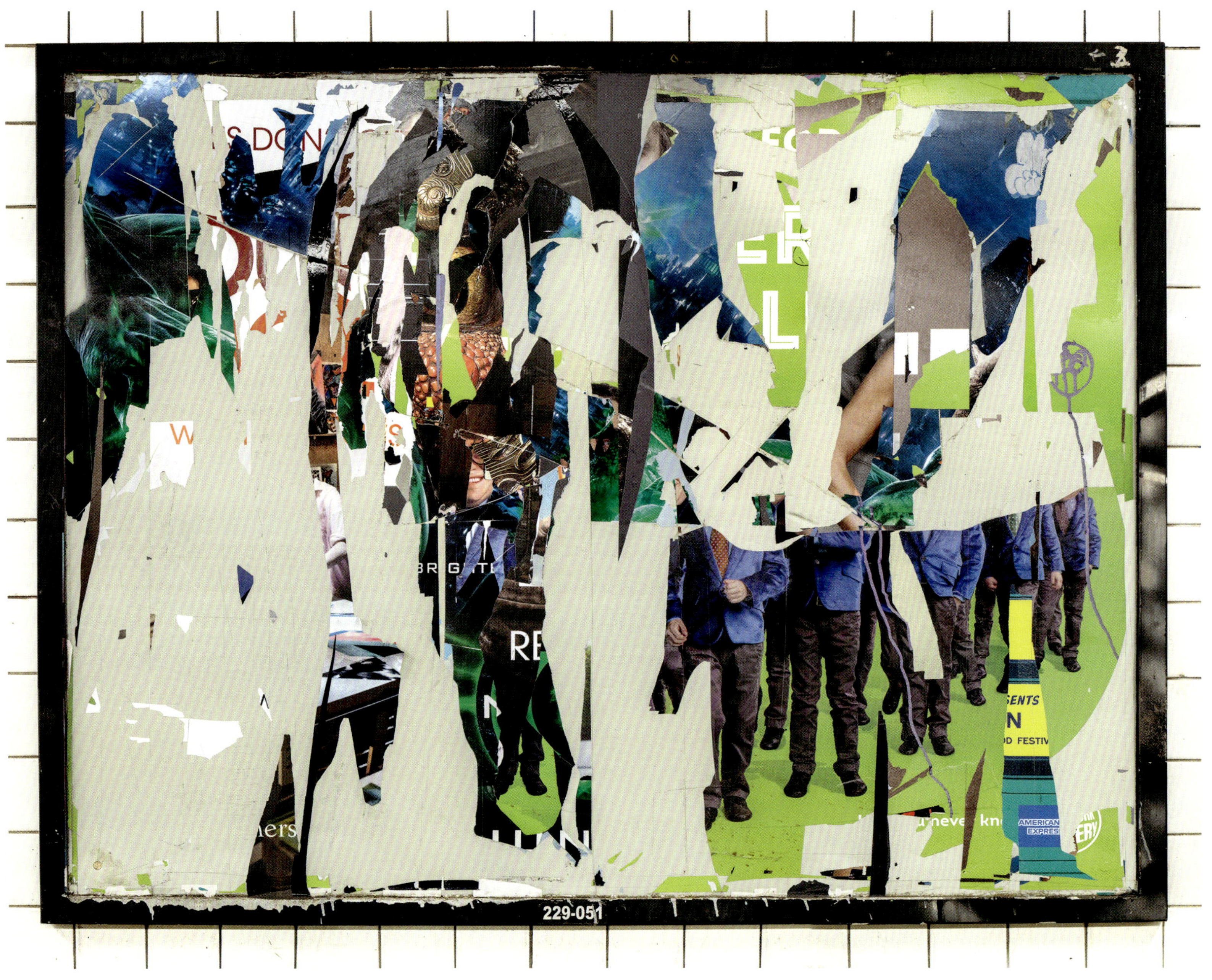
229-051

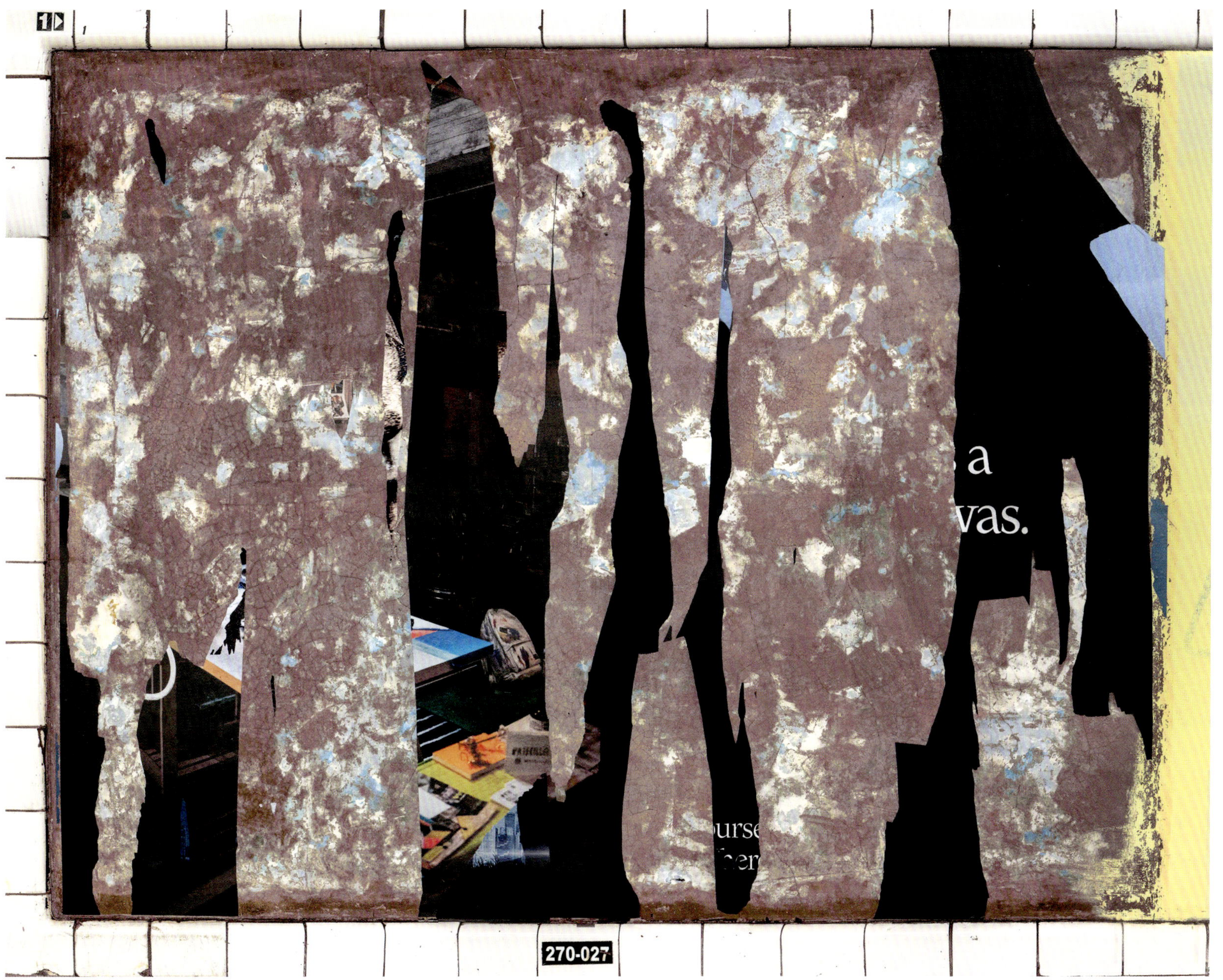
a
vas.
270-027

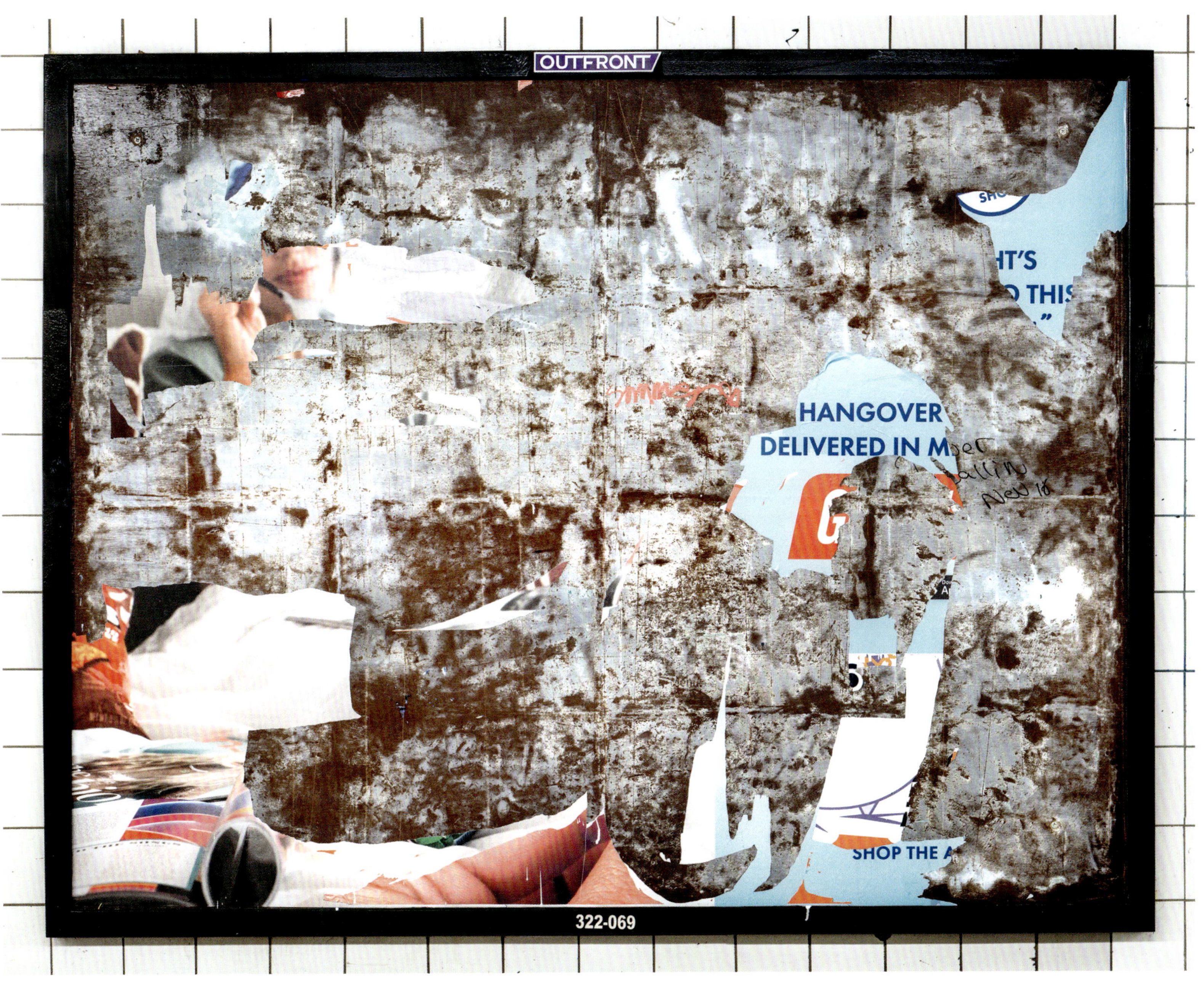
OUTFRONT
SHO
HT'S
O THIS
"
HANGOVER
DELIVERED IN M
G
SHOP THE A
322-069

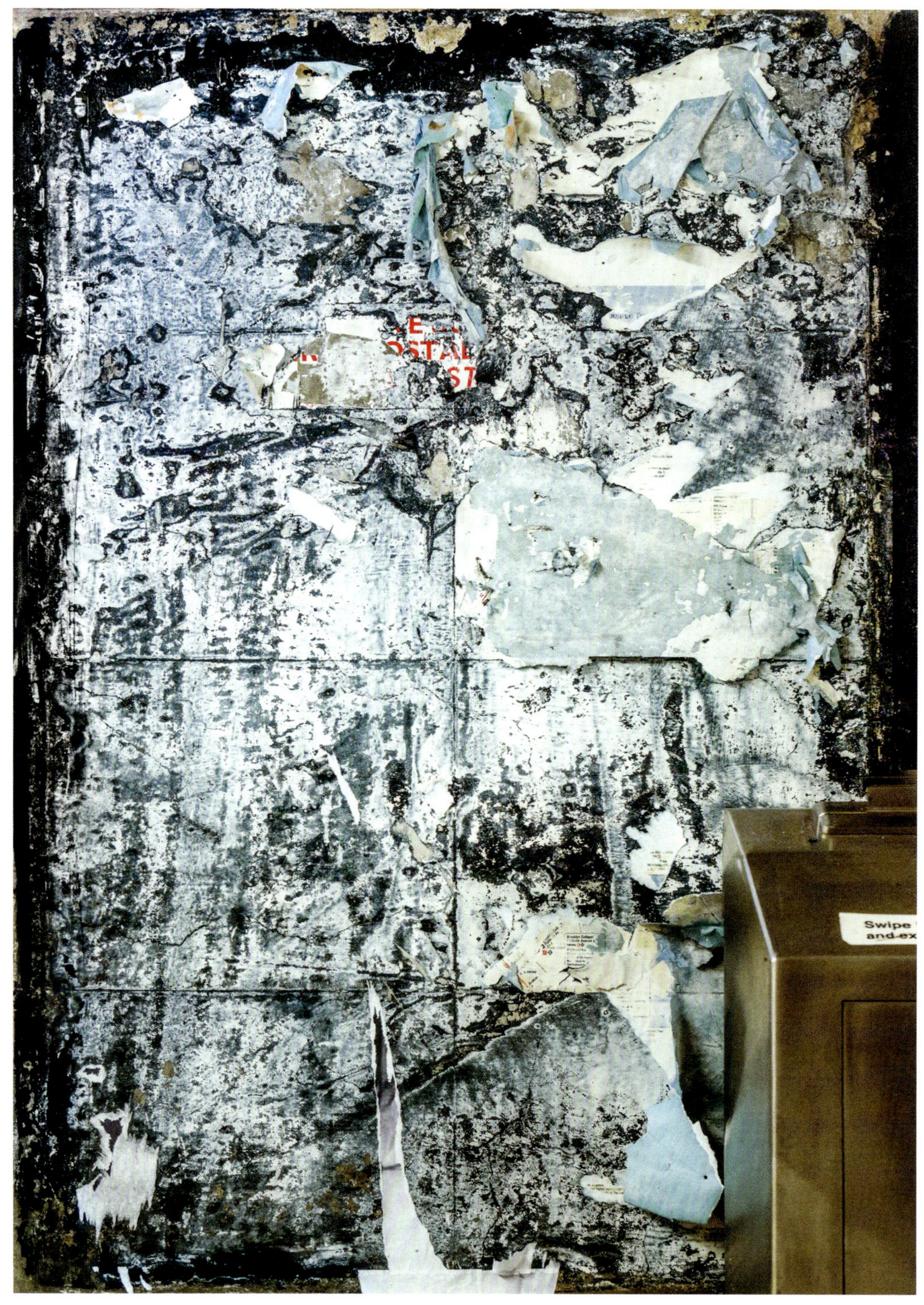

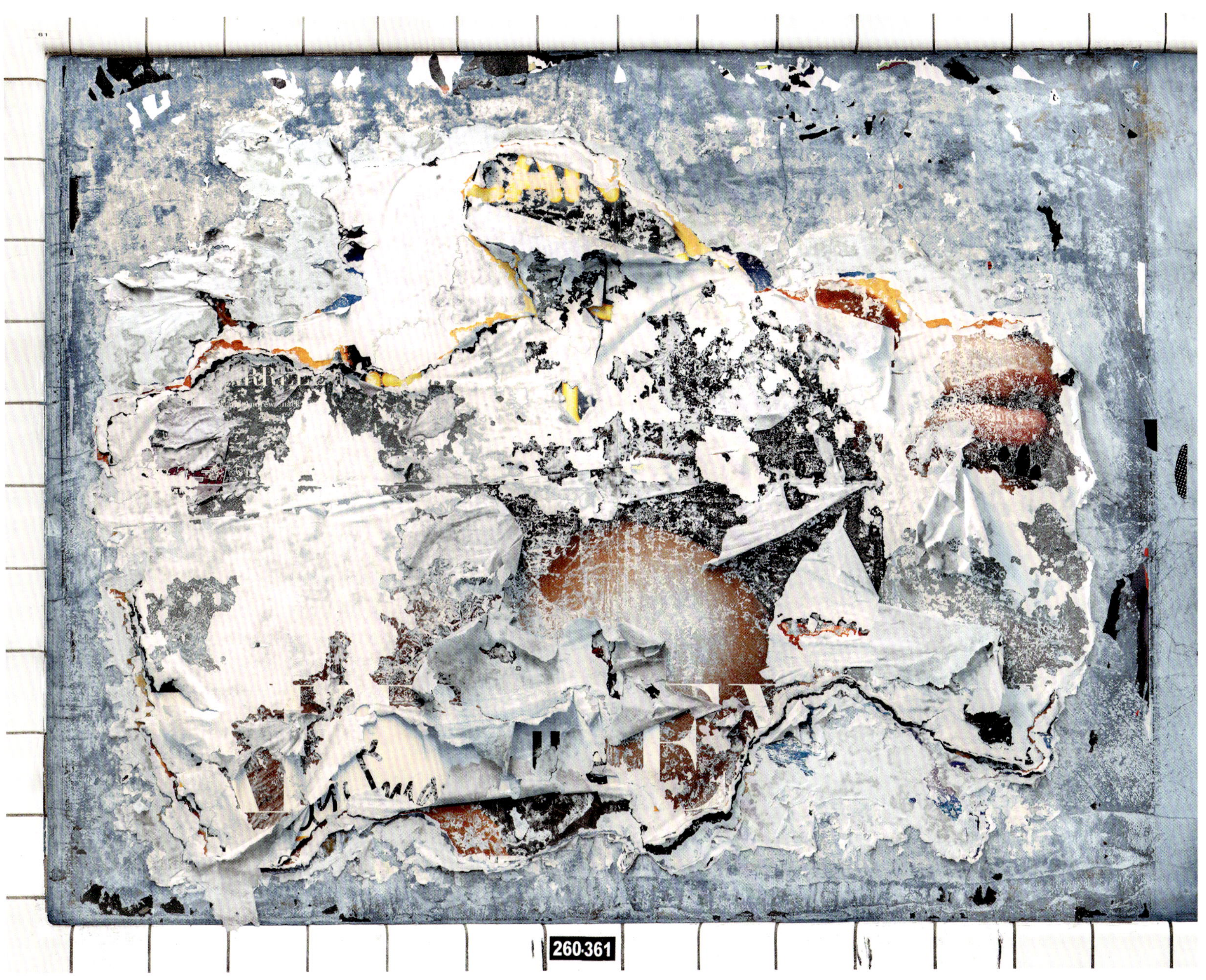

260·361

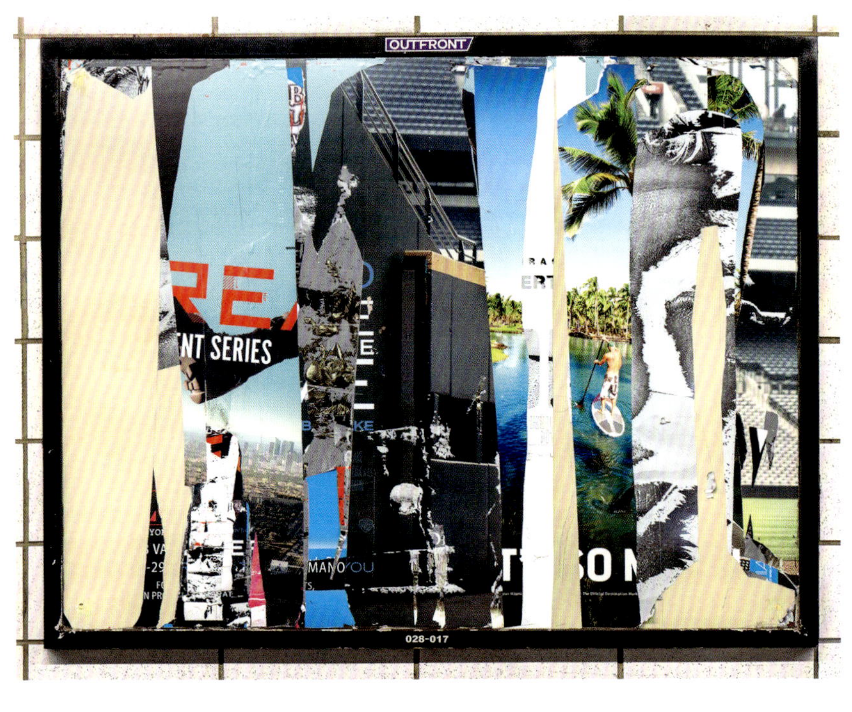

OUTFRONT
028-017

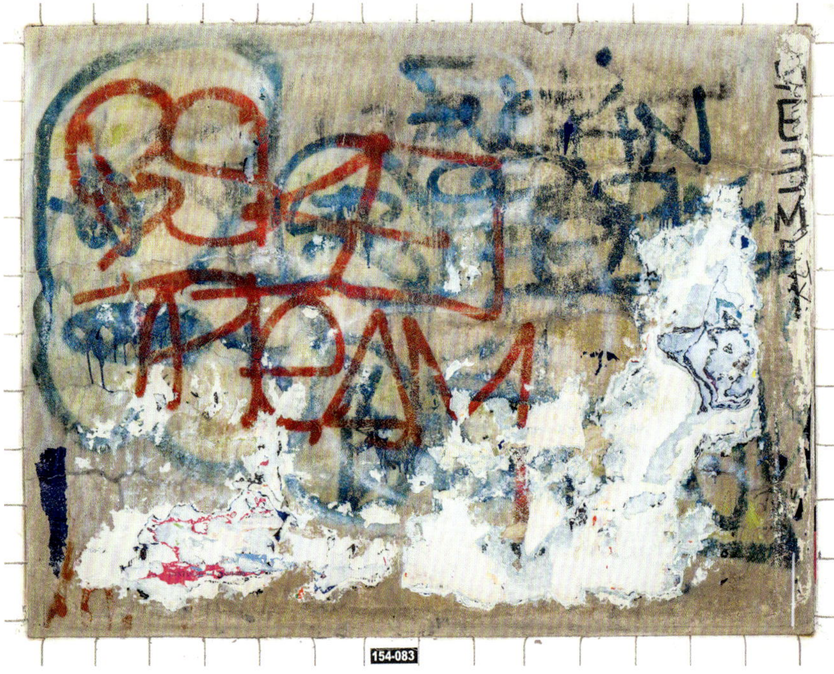

154-083

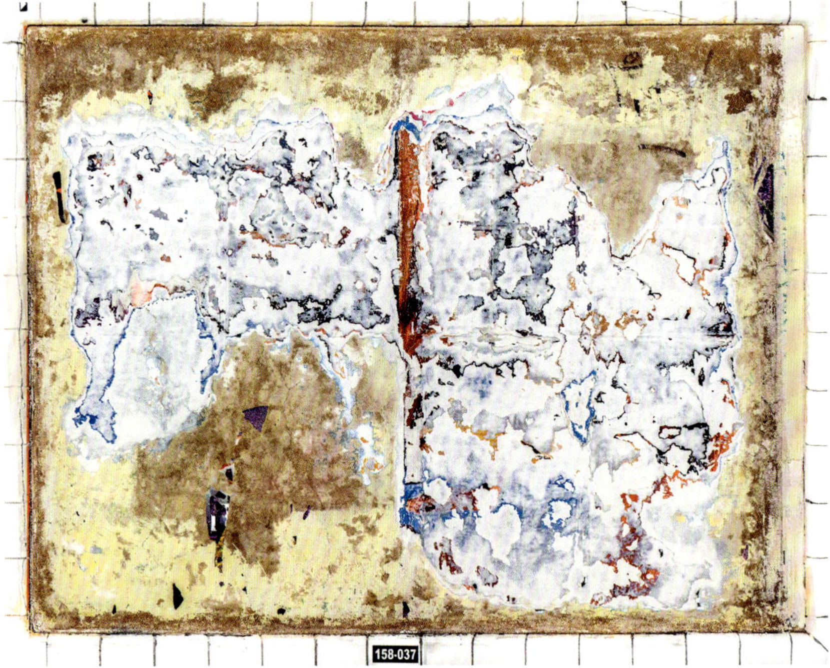

158-037

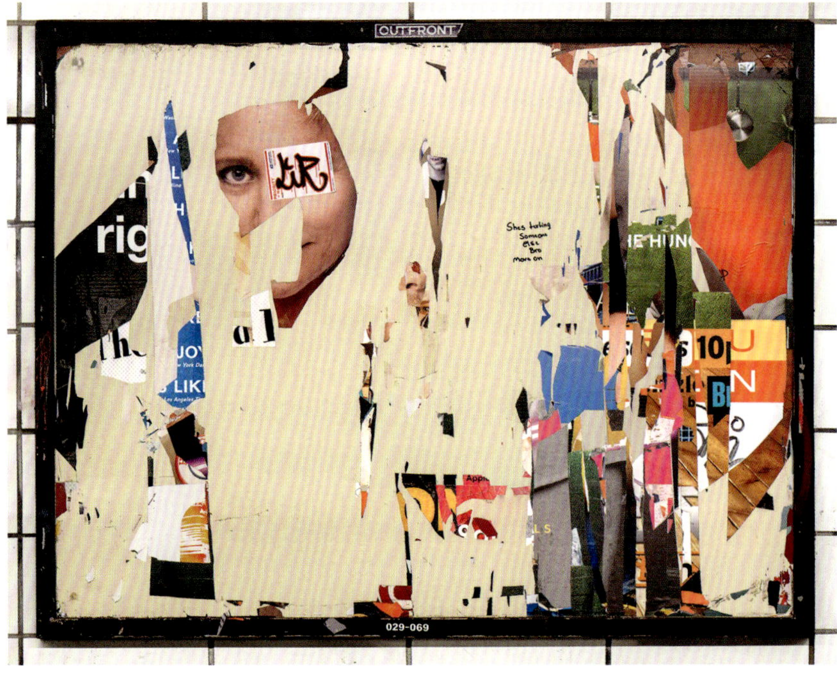

OUTFRONT
029-069

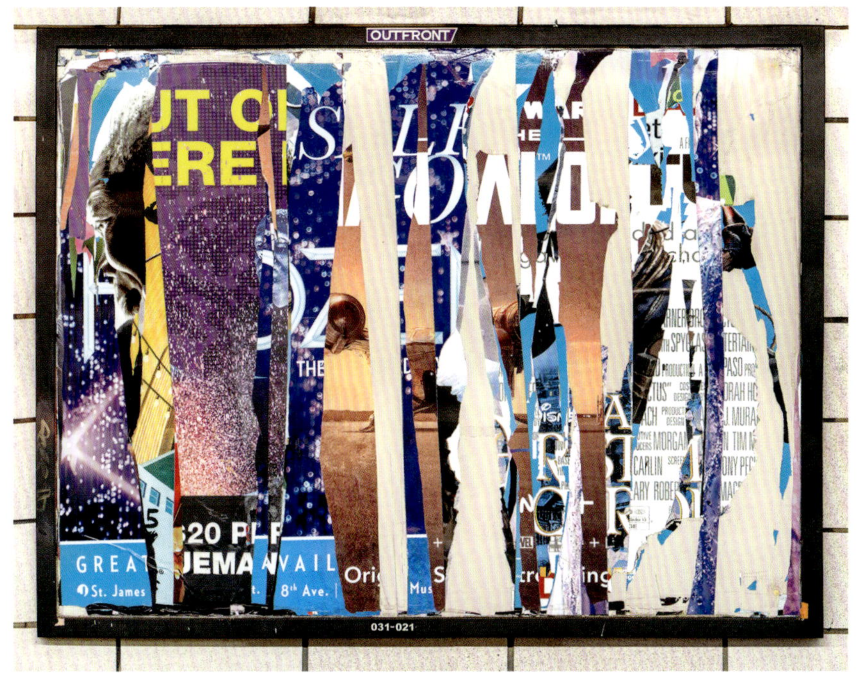
OUTFRONT
UT O
ERE
GREAT
St. James
8th Ave.
031-021

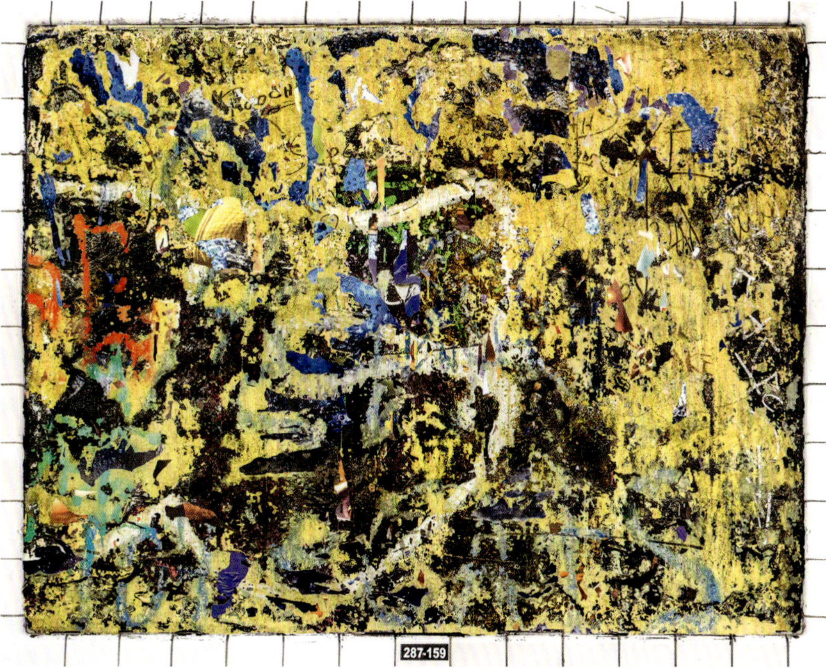
287-159

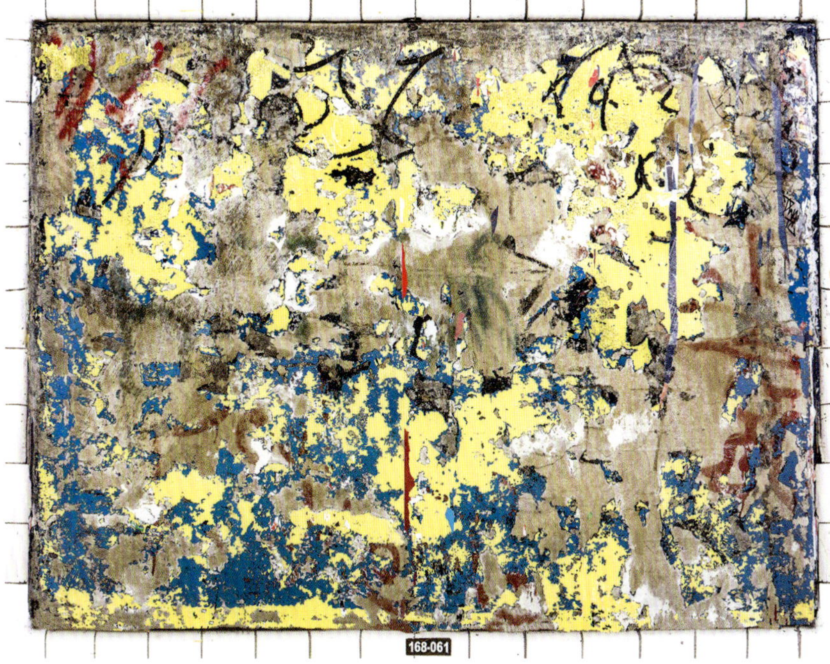
168-061

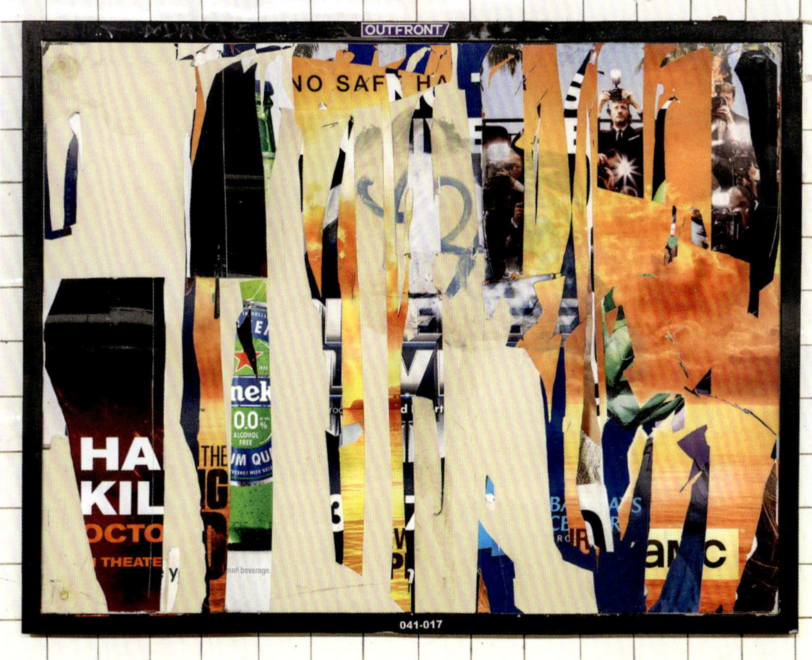
OUTFRONT
NO SAF
HA
KIL
OCTO
THEATE
041-017

Plate List

P. 86   wall cut, 231-141, Grand St., IND Sixth Ave. Line, New York, NY

P. 88   wall cut, 237-147, Carroll St., IND Culver Line, Brooklyn, NY

P. 89–90   wall cut, 237-207 – 237-211, Carroll St., IND Culver Line, Brooklyn, NY

P. 91   wall cut, 217-157, 170th St., IND Concourse Line, Bronx, NY

P. 94   wall cut, 289-003, Bedford-Nostrand Aves., IND Crosstown Line, Brooklyn, NY

P. 95   wall cut, 409-041, Spring St., IRT Lexington Ave. Line, New York, NY

P. 96   wall cut, 409-011, Spring St., IRT Lexington Ave. Line, New York, NY

P. 97–98   wall cut, 214-205 – 214-209, 182nd-183rd Sts., IND Concourse Line, Bronx, NY

P. 100   wall cut, 284-163, Nassau Ave., IND Crosstown Line, Brooklyn, NY

P. 101   wall cut, 214-229, 182nd-183rd Sts., IND Concourse Line, Bronx, NY

P. 103–105 wall cut, 162-143 – 162-147, 50th St., IND Eighth Ave. Line, New York, NY

P. 108   wall cut, Casino, 103rd St., IND Eighth Ave. Line, New York, NY

P. 109   wall cut, 229-051, 14th St.-6th Ave., IND Sixth Ave. Line, New York, NY

P. 110   wall cut, 270-027, 46th St., IND Queens Blvd. Line, Queens, NY

P. 112   wall cut, 322-069, 14th St.-6th Ave., New York, NY

P. 113   wall cut, unnumbered, Court Sq.-23rd St., IND Crosstown Line, Queens, NY

P. 116   wall cut, 260-361, 75th Ave., IND Queens Blvd. Line, Queens, NY

P. 117, clockwise from top left:

        wall cut, 028-017, Union St., BMT Fourth Ave. Line, Brooklyn, NY

        wall cut, 154-083, 116th St., IND Eighth Ave. Line, New York, NY

        wall cut, 029-069, 4th Ave. & 9th St., BMT Fourth Ave. Line, Brooklyn, NY

        wall cut, 158-037, 86th St., IND Eighth Ave. Line, New York, NY

P. 118, clockwise from top left:

        wall cut, 031-021, 25th St., BMT Fourth Ave. Line, Brooklyn, NY

        wall cut, 287-159, Flushing Ave., IND Crosstown Line, Brooklyn, NY

        wall cut, 041-017, Seventh Ave., BMT Brighton Line, Brooklyn, NY

        wall cut, 168-061, Spring St., IND Eighth Ave. Line, New York, NY

P. 125   construction fence, 25th St. between 10th & 11th Aves., New York, NY

Acknowledgments

I would like to acknowledge the following, without whom this book would not be possible:

My parents, Sherry Ceniza and Jim Lewis, who encouraged my artistic pursuits from an early age, and instilled in me a sense of limitless possibility.

My sister, Shawn Lewis, whose wise counsel anticipated applications for my work before I was daring enough to pursue them.

My friends, whose engagement with my work has been sustaining and affirming: Sam Altekruse, Lisa Bender, Jane Huth, Morgan Powell, Anita Provost, Anthony Rebholz, Lindsey Roberts, Lorna Schofield, and Rodney Walker.

The anonymous street artists who made these works a truly collaborative effort.

The team at Daylight Books: Michael Itkoff, for his vision for the book; and Ursula Damm, for making that vision a reality.

Kathleen Hulser, for her wise and generous words.

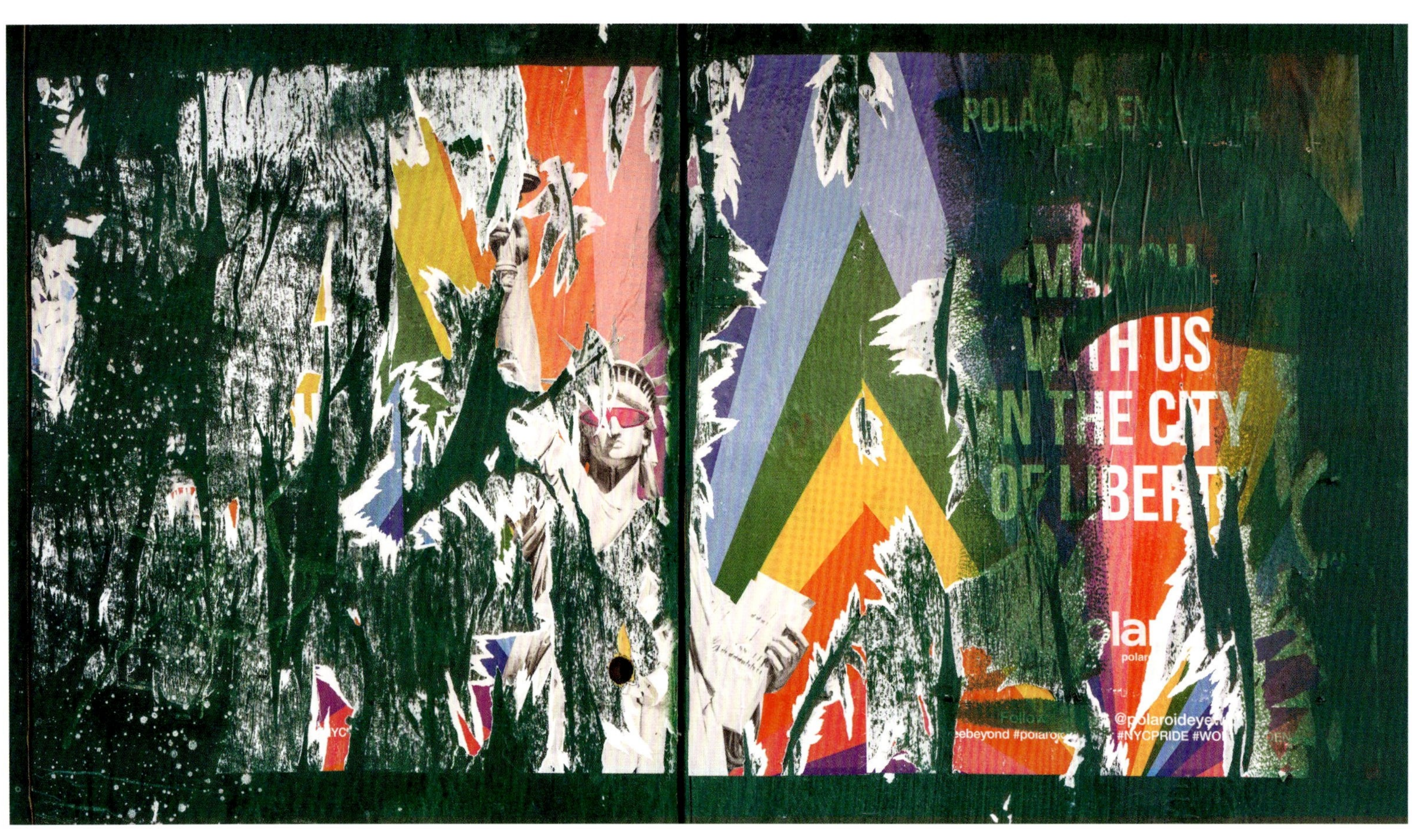

POLAROID
WITH US
IN THE CITY
OF LIBERTY
@polaroideye
#NYCPRIDE #WO
NYC

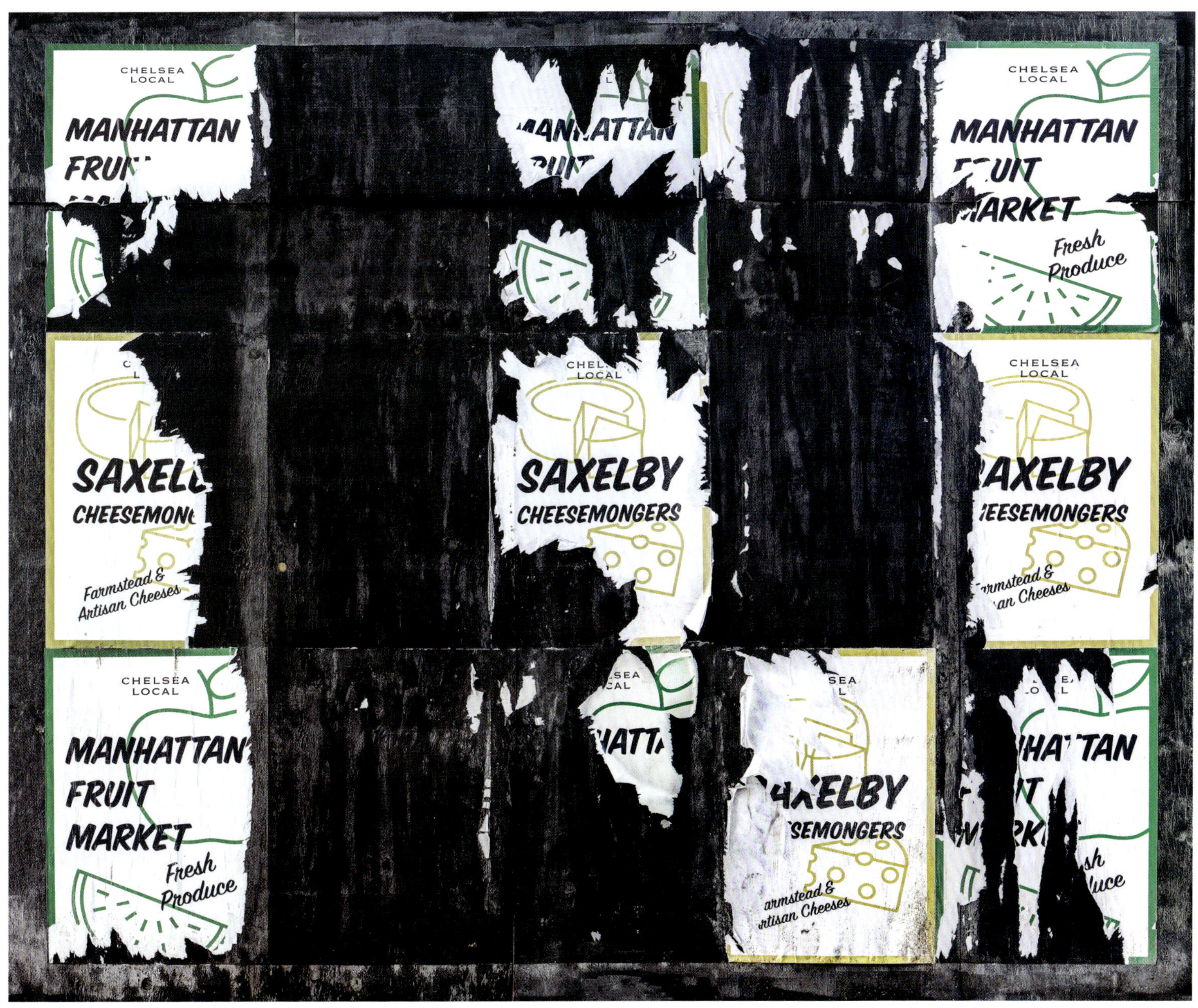

CHELSEA LOCAL
MANHATTAN FRUIT MARKET
CHELSEA LOCAL
MANHATTAN FRUIT MARKET
Fresh Produce
SAXELBY CHEESEMONGERS
Farmstead & Artisan Cheeses
SAXELBY CHEESEMONGERS
CHELSEA LOCAL
SAXELBY CHEESEMONGERS
Farmstead & Artisan Cheeses
CHELSEA LOCAL
MANHATTAN FRUIT MARKET
Fresh Produce
SAXELBY CHEESEMONGERS
Farmstead & Artisan Cheeses
MANHATTAN FRUIT MARKET

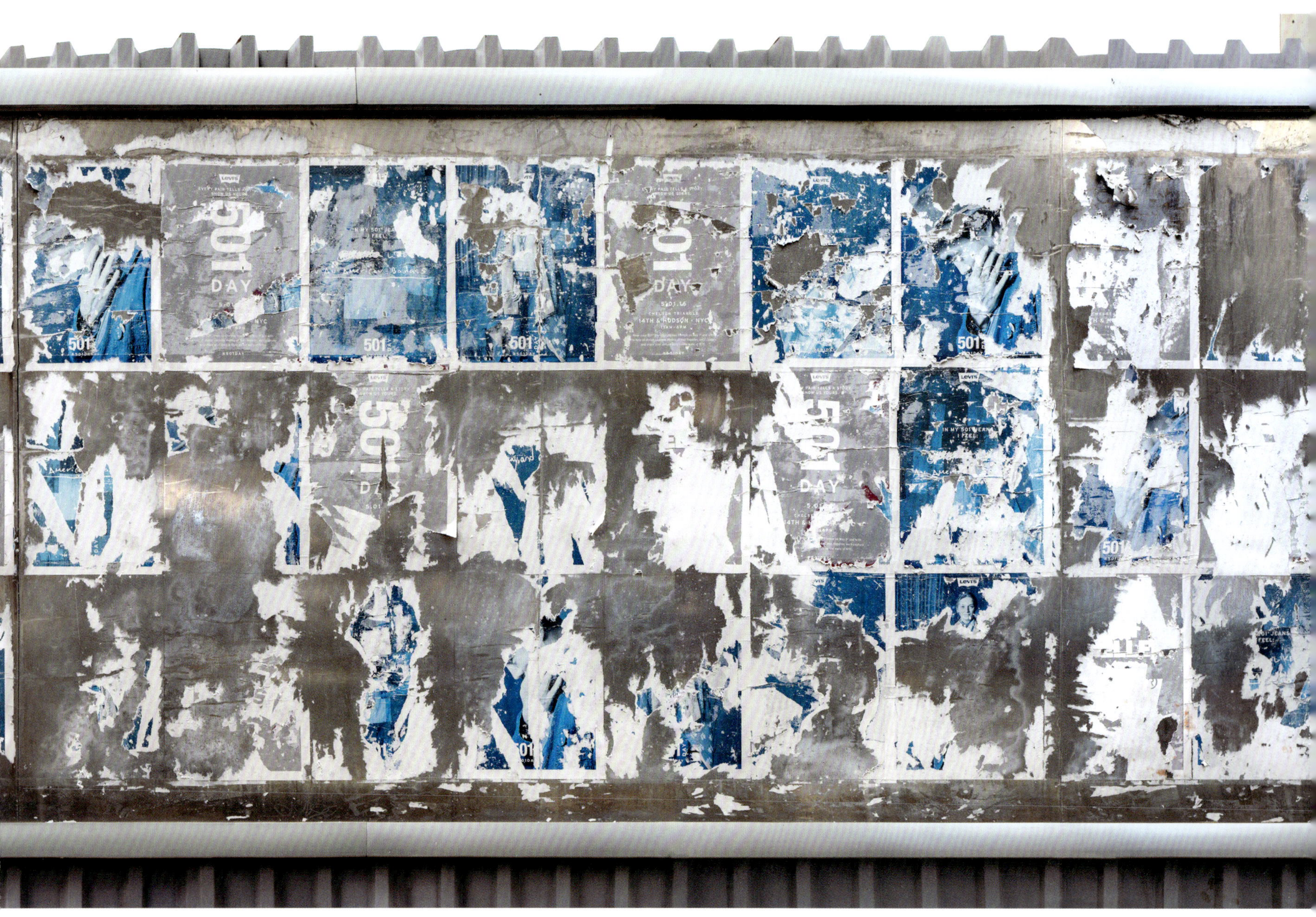

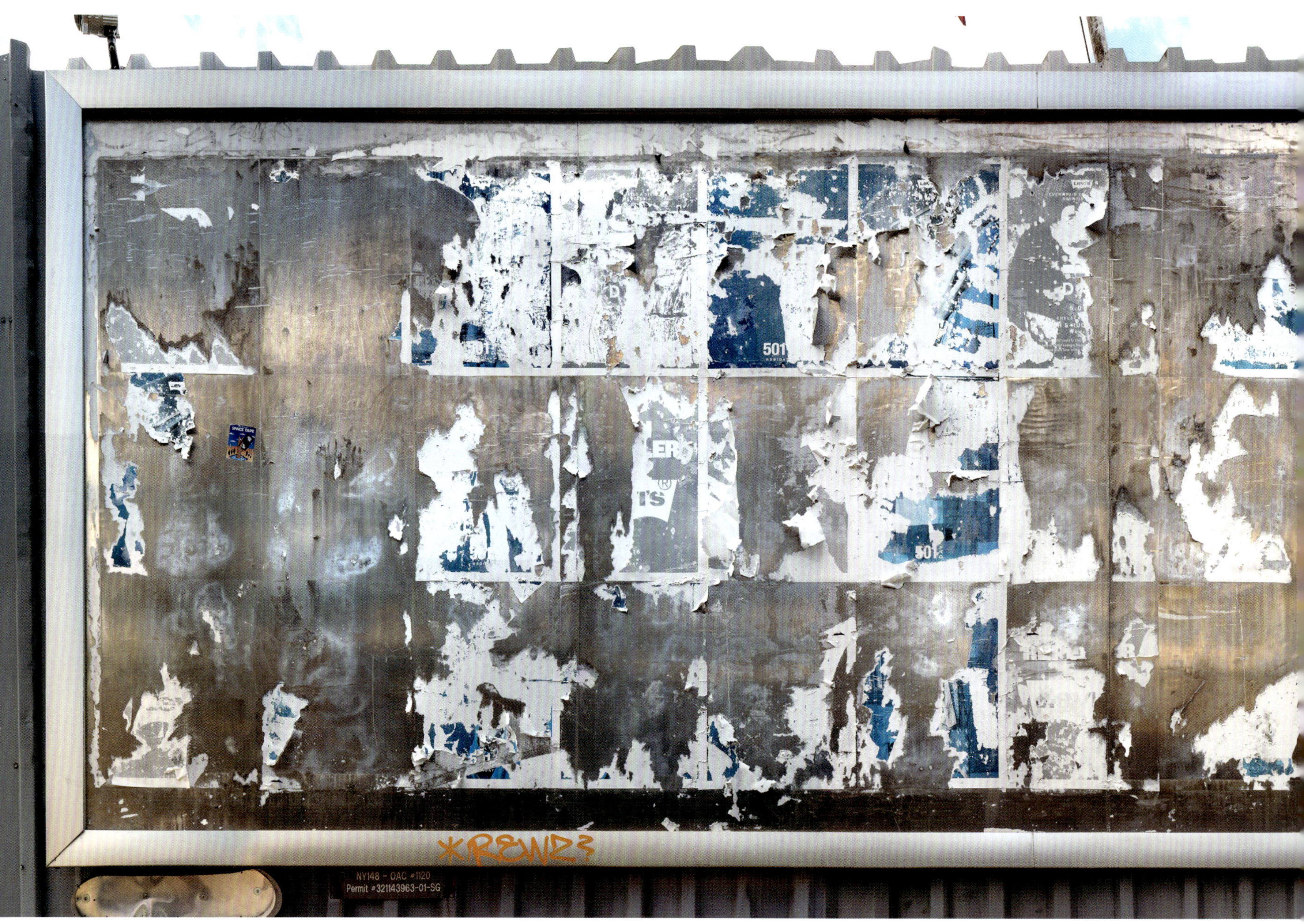
501
501
NY148 - OAC #1120
Permit #321143963-01-SG

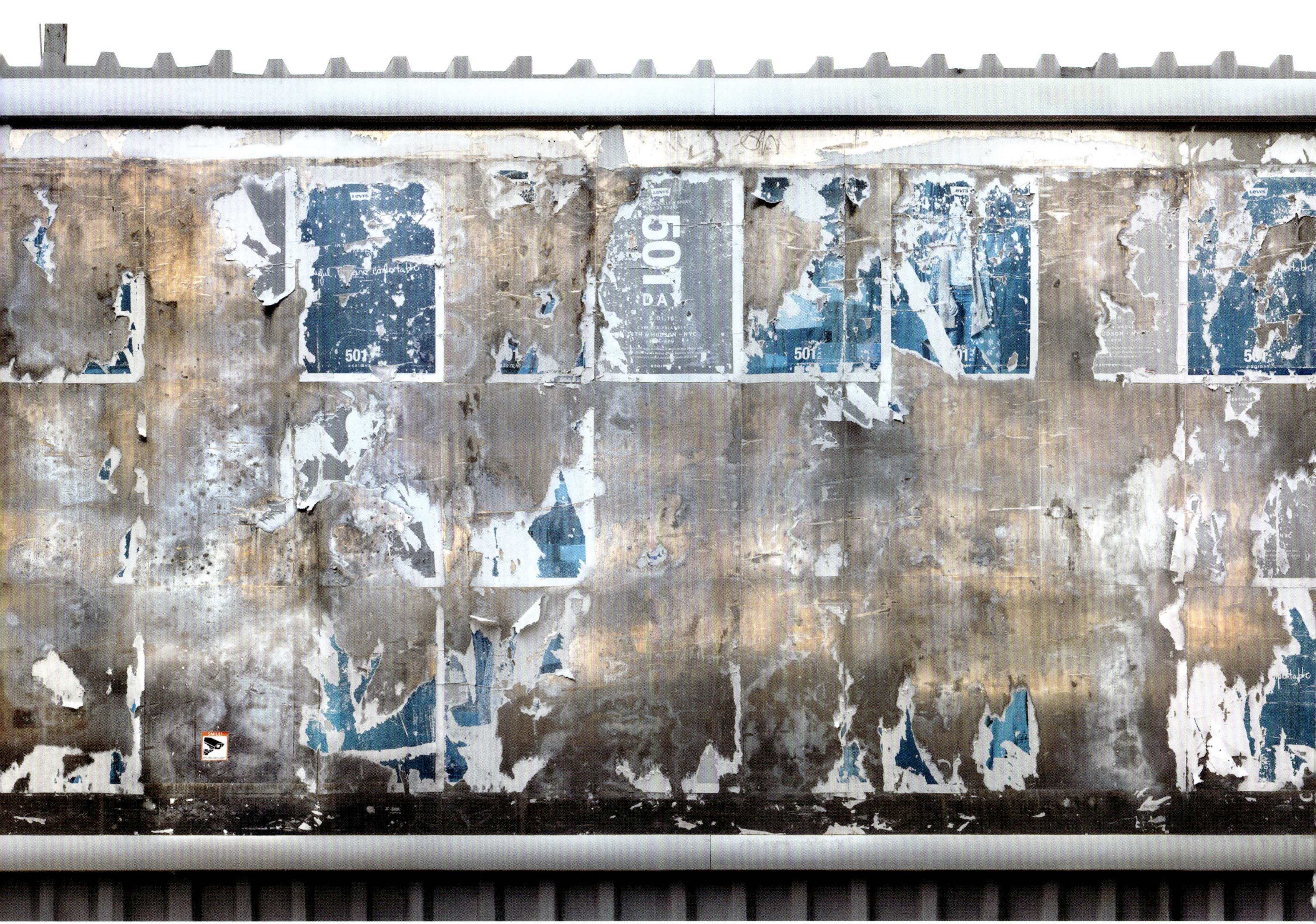

Post No Bills:
Art and Advertising on the Street

by Kathleen Hulser

Our world is layered; why not peel it back? *The Many Pleasures* celebrates the irresistible urge to find and make art of our everyday surroundings, a pastime that flourishes in neighborhoods with abandoned buildings useful only as billboard stands, construction projects enclosed by green fences, and the ad-lined corridors of subway stations. Barton Lewis's closely observed advertising posters, altered by weathering but more often by strategic slashing, tearing, and scribbling, document widespread creative impulses. Engagement in the city brings out the artist in everyone. Lewis embraces the casual visual encounters that constitute the exciting realm of street art, far from the gallery and museum but close to the eyes of the urban stroller. In subway stations the white tiles frame the art, a natural gallery constantly altered with new and deteriorated ads, and intentionally defaced posters. Here tension crackles between accidental weathering and deliberate alterations practiced by insomniac would-be artists armed with box cutters, scrapers, and Sharpies. Lewis's current collection comes in two series: *Wall Cuts* and *Urban Topographies*, the latter including relay mailboxes, building facades, and construction fences.

Born in Illinois, Barton Lewis is a slim, vigorous Brooklynite who enjoys New York City's varied streetscapes. Highly observant, with oodles of photographic chops, he laser focuses on phenomena that usually have a subliminal impact. He adopts the code of the flaneûr, those cosmopolitan observers of the city. As the poet Charles Baudelaire wrote, "For the perfect flâneur, for the passionate spectator, it is an immense joy to set up house in the heart of the multitude, amid the ebb and flow of movement, in the midst of the fugitive and the infinite." Lewis's own fascination with art and randomness has led him to prowl the city in search of inadvertent art including advertising stands, mailboxes, construction fences, doorways, gates, and vintage signs.

Originally a filmmaker, he shot the short film *wall cuts, train stations, New York City* on his classic Arriflex Super 16 camera. He edited his footage at Millennium Film Workshop in the East Village, long a mecca for experimental filmmakers, run for forty years by Howard Guttenplan, honored at the end of the film. Giants of the avant-garde such as Michael Snow, Yvonne Rainer, Ken Jacobs, and Carolee

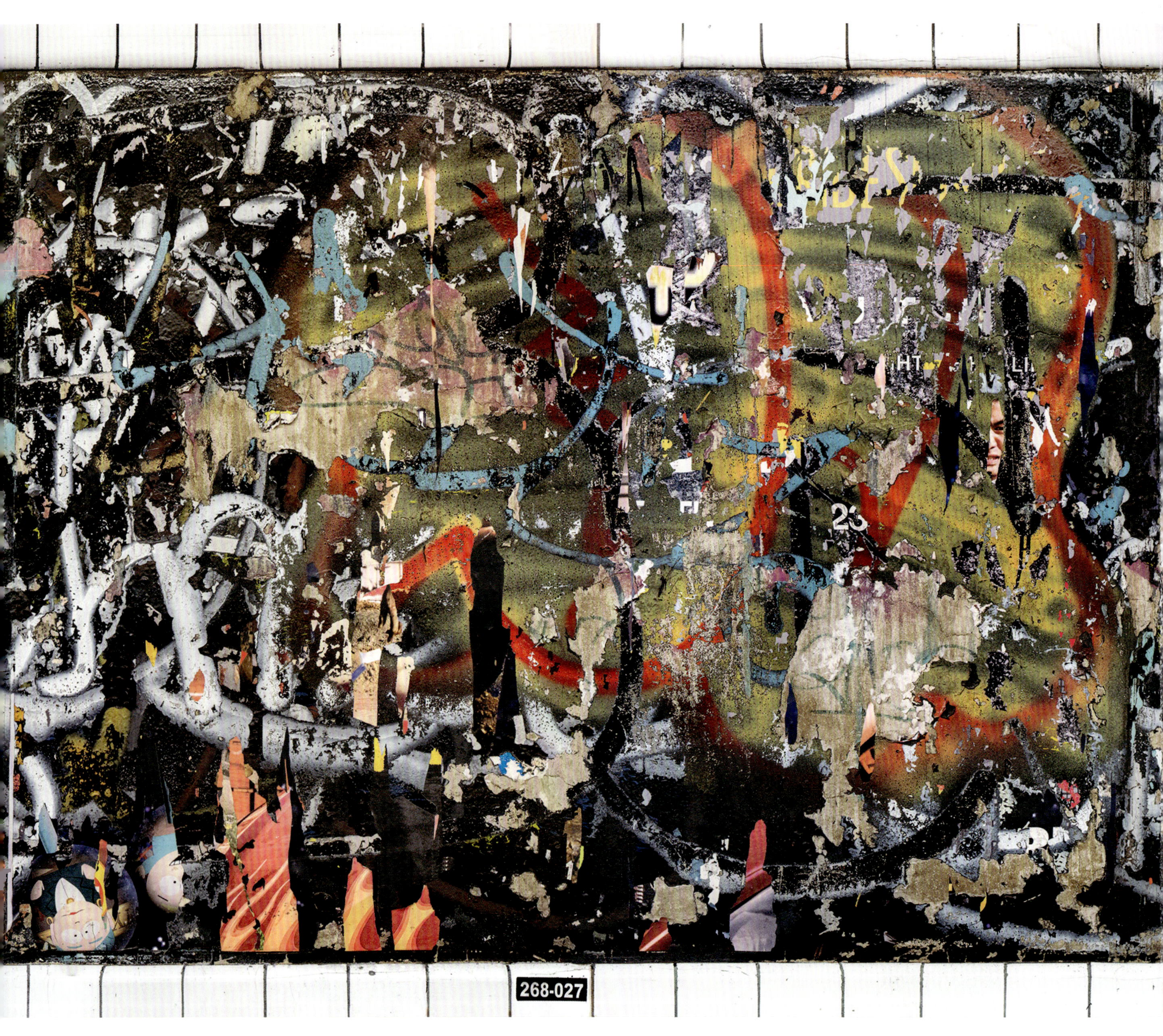

268-027

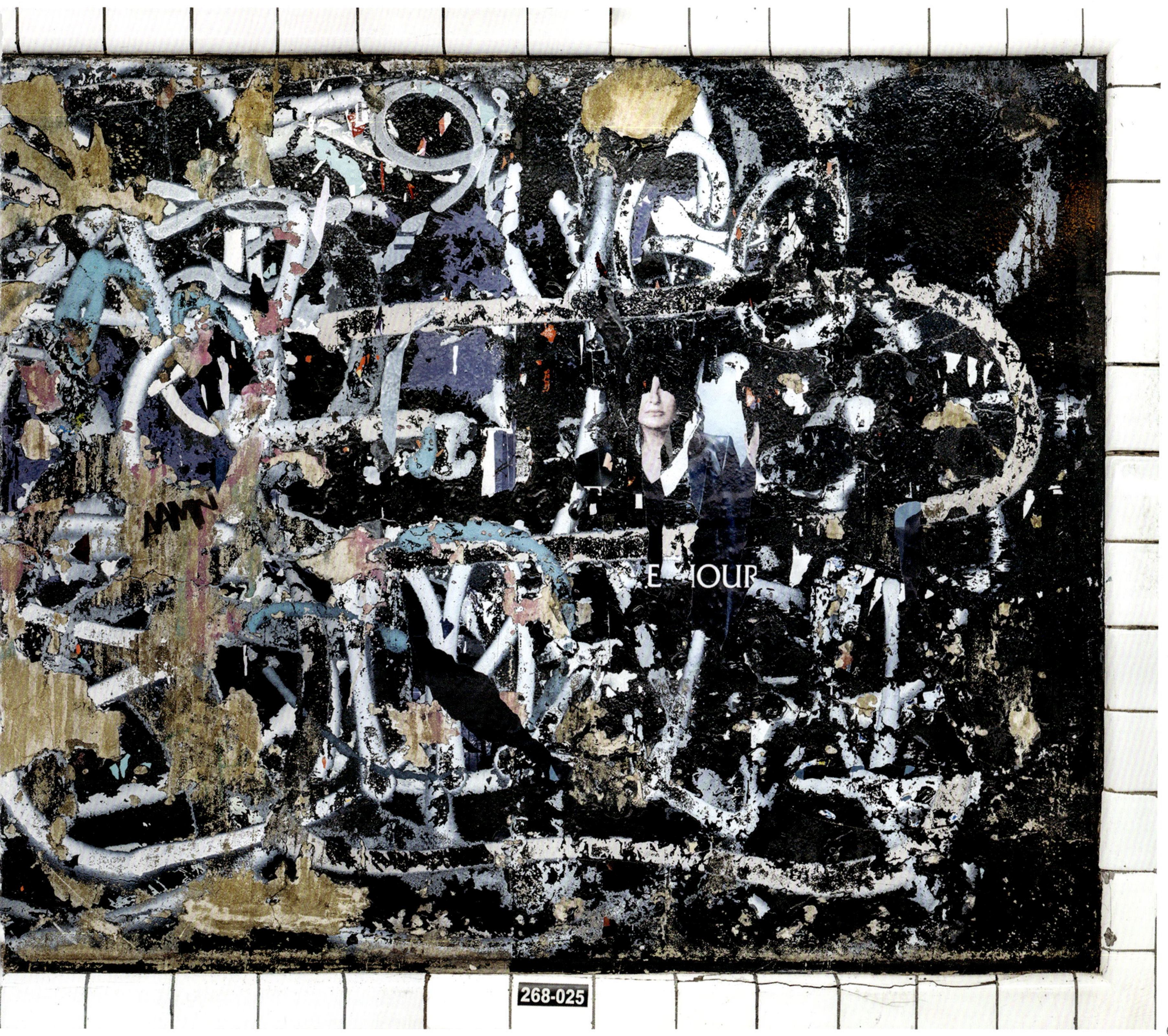
E OUR